History of the Lehigh Coal and Navigation Company Series:

Summit Hill and Panther Creek Operations & the Switch-Back Railroad

Vince Hydro

Published by: Vince Hydro
Jim Thorpe, Pennsylvania

Copyright © 2022 by Vince Hydro

Published by Vince Hydro
vincent.hydro@gmail.com

Layout by Vince Hydro

Also by Vince Hydro:
➢ *The Mauch Chunk Switchback, America's Pioneer Railroad* © 2002.
➢ *History of the Lehigh Coal and Navigation Company's Room Run Railroad* © 2019.
➢ *Asa Packer's People, The Story of the Packer Children: Lucy, Mary, Robert and Harry-their Lives and Legacies* © 2020
➢ *Mauch Chunk History Series: America's First Roller-Coaster. The Summit Hill & Mauch Chunk Gravity Railroad & Switchback* © 2022

ISBN 978-1-7923-9553-6

Library of Congress Control Number: 2022913447

Printed by
Christmas City Printing Co
Bethlehem, PA 18018

Front Cover Illustration:
A young miner poses in the entrance to Panther Valley coal mine Tunnel No. 8 for photographer M.A. Kleckner circa 1870. These images were used in stereopticon viewers and were sold in Mauch Chunk and at other tourist sites.

Rear Cover Illustration:
Slatepickers pose for M.A. Kleckner, who shot his 1870 stereopticon series, "A Trip Around the Switchback" primarily in the Panther Creek Valley. This shanty was located near coal breaker No. 8, at the western end of the Valley. The LC&N used young boys and older men, those not capable of working in the dusty underground mines, as slatepickers in its mechanized coal breakers. These "breaker boys" often posed for the tourists who passed through the Panther Creek Valley on their "Trip Around the Switchback."

Dedication

This book is dedicated to the late William T. "Bill" Richards (1910-1994) long-time resident of the Panther Creek Valley, who, following his retirement in 1971 became the recognized, leading historian of Lansford and the Panther Creek Valley.

Bill was a frequent contributor to Lansford's *Valley Gazette* newspaper, published by the late Edward Gildea. I became acquainted with Bill through his articles in the *Gazette*, and then was personally introduced to him by Harry Murphy, another Valley resident and self-taught historian. When I began my first paper for the Canal History and Technology Symposium and Proceedings in 1990, Bill was an invaluable mentor, and allowed me access to maps and papers in his collection.

I spent many hours visiting with Bill, Ed Gildea and Harry Murphy, poring over old photos and documents, and discussing aspects of local history, including the history of the Panther Valley and the Lehigh Coal and Navigation Company (hereinafter LC&N). Much of the understanding I gained from discussions with Bill went into a later paper that I presented at the Canal History and Technology Symposium in the year 2000, on the LC&N's Panther Creek Operations. That paper provided much of the basis for this current publication.

Bill's mentoring went beyond local history and included advice for speaking in public. My presentation at the Symposium was my first real public speaking experience on history. With trepidation, being an amateur historian facing a veritable sea of degreed academics, I was nervous, but able to proceed with the help of Bill's valuable advice.

When Bill passed away in 1994, Ed Gildea said it best, in a commentary in the May 1994 issue of the *Valley Gazette*:

Bill Richards—historian, mentor, friend

Bill Richards died after an extended illness on Sunday, April 24, at Miners Memorial Medical Center in Coaldale at the age of 83 and the feeling here is one of irreplaceable loss.

It's one of those things that you probably should have prepared for, but didn't.

Bill joined the Gazette team early-on and shared everything he knew about the Panther Valley area's past.

He kept a printed sign on the door of his home at 45 Center Street in Lansford which said "Ring bell Walk in."

Many people went there with questions about the past and about their roots and Bill received them graciously and helped them, even while he was bedfast for many months.

He was a teacher, athlete, outdoorsman, craftsman, soldier, a leader of men and boys, a mentor and, above all, a historian who spoke about our past and showed slides from a collection amassed over the years.

He was a man whose measure can't be taken in a few paragraphs.

Most of all, he was a valued friend. We'll have more about him from our own standpoint and from others who knew him.

William T. Richards is survived by his daughter, Elizabeth Lynn, and his brother, George Brinley, and, for now, we can only join his family and his many friends in mourning our loss. ##

Bill Richards (right) and the late Pete Schmauch confer on a Panther Valley hillside during one of their many explorations of the valley's railroad and mining system. Reprinted from the February 1979 issue of Lansford's *Valley Gazette* newspaper.

Preface & Acknowledgements

This work is a complete rewrite of a similar history I wrote 22 years ago. This book completely supersedes that earlier paper, which was written for the Canal History and Technology Symposium Proceedings, Volume XIX, published on March 18, 2000. Material in this book also supersedes what I wrote in Chapter 5 of my 2002 work: *The Mauch Chunk Switchback: America's Pioneer Railroad.*

The story of the LC&N mining and railroad operations in Summit Hill and the Panther Valley is a complex tale, of a constantly changing system facing innumerable challenges. To present a comprehensible picture of the area history, I have limited the scope to the time preceding and up to the year 1873. At least one other book, and perhaps several would be needed to cover the history after this point. However, Julian Parton's *The Death of a Great Company* contains an excellent history of the Summit Hill and Panther Valley mines in the later years. I have also limited the western extent of this book's scope to Tunnel No. 10. The story of the collieries further west, including those operated by the LC&N will be told later.

As with all my work, numerous individuals provided reference materials, photos and invaluable insights. I would like to especially acknowledge Christopher Northington for his research and insight into the etymology of the term, "switch-back" regarding railroad operations. According to his investigations, the English word, "Switch-Back" came into use because of the fame of the Panther Valley section of the Summit Hill and Mauch Chunk Gravity Railroad. (See Appendix B.)

Appreciation is also extended to the following:

- BJ Berk for use of the Map of Ashton
- Alex Japha, Lehigh University, Chapman Sketch of the Great Mine
- Martha Capwell Fox, National Canal Museum in Easton for use of photographs
- Harry Murphy, for clues to the use of locomotives within the Valley, and operation of "lead-in" tracks at the foot of Panther Creek Inclined Planes
- Jerry Hoare, use of the Slatepicker's Shanty photograph
- Bob Gormley, for access and use of phtographs from his extensive collection
- Pete DiMatia, for feeding me photographs and tidbits of interesting Valley history and exploration and tours of sites with historical interest
- National Canal Museum of Easton, photographs and access to diaries of Robert Heysham Sayre
- Dave Kuchta, Tunnel No. 3 photo
- Walt Nieoff, for communication and insight into PV switch operation
- Luzerne County Historical Society, photos and sketches
- Dimmick Memorial Library, use of microfilmed newspapers
- Mauch Chunk Museum and Culural Center
- Panther Valley No. 9 Mine Museum, photo of Fisher Hazard

v

"The change from one track to the other is made by a curious and Ingenious self-acting arrangement, from which the entire road on this descent, from the Summit to Panther Creek, takes its name of the Switch-Back Railroad." MS Henry, 1860

The Unknown Valley

PANTHER CREEK VALLEY, located in central-eastern Pennsylvania, is presently populated by the old coal mining boroughs of Lansford and Coaldale, each at one time a mixture of small mining hamlets or "patches," that once made up the eastern end of the Southern Anthracite Coal Field. The Valley lies within a narrow, east-west triangle of land, enclosed on the west by the borough of Tamaqua, on the east by the Lehigh River; by Sharp Mountain on the south, and by the Locust or Nesquehoning Mountain on the north. These ranges converge at Mount Pisgah in the east and diverge as they head west.

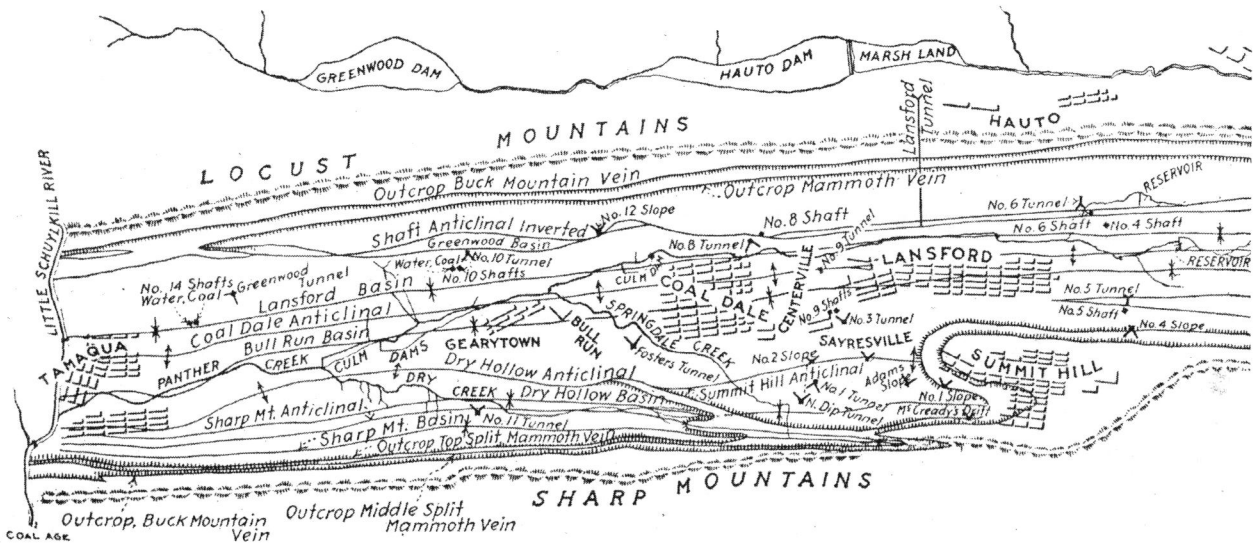

These two maps show the triangle of land encompassing the Panther Valley and Room Run (Nesquehoning) mines. From *Coal Age Magazine*, 10 May 1913

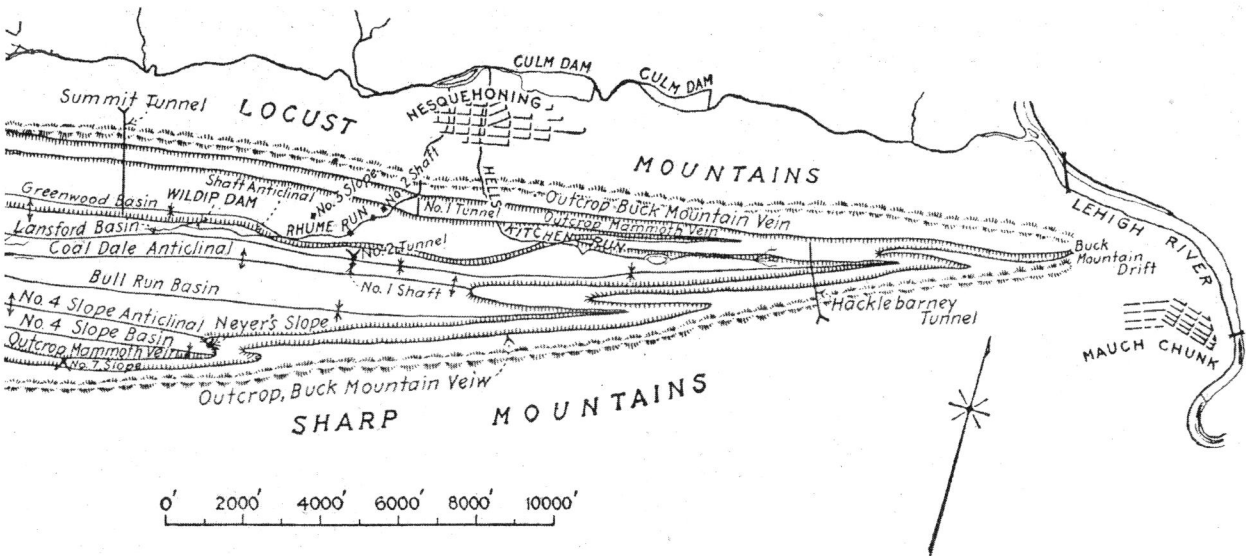

When the United States of America separated from Great Britain, this area, located as it is beyond the Blue Mountain in Pennsylvania, was a wilderness frontier, traversed only by Native Americans, and those motivated missionaries seeking converts to the North. Within a half-century following our Declaration of Independence, that all would change, and the Panther Creek Valley would become one of the major anthracite coal producing regions in America.

1

Earliest Settlers

SOME OF THE EARLIEST settlers in this part of Pennsylvania were the Moravians, a religious sect that purchased land near the mouth of the Mahoning Creek, along the Lehigh River, and established a mission for Native Americans converted to the Christian Faith. This settlement was known as Gnaden-Hutten and was located near the site of present-day Weissport.

The next settlers of interest to our story were two men, Jacob Weiss and Philip Ginder. History records that in 1783 Weiss, having retired from his service in George Washington's Continental Army, bought a tract of land from the Moravians at present-day Weissport. This sect, headquartered in Bethlehem, in 1747-1748 had constructed a road leading to the area from Bethlehem.[1] Two years later Weiss loaded up his possessions, and with his family, settled along the Lehigh River at present-day Weissport. Weiss quickly established himself as a farmer and lumberman, sending lumber and other commodities to downstream markets, probably the first person to do so.[2]

Jacob Weiss' place in local history is well documented. Although no definitive book-length history has yet been written about him, numerous historical societies and archives preserve records of his life and activities.

The life and legacy of Philip Ginder (aka Ginter) is less well-known. At this time there are two main sources of information on this man; the first was written Dr. Thomas Chalkley James, a Philadelphia obstetrician, and the second by folklorist George Korson, who penned a well-researched and highly readable account of Ginder in *Black Rock*.

Col. Jacob Weiss (1748-1838)

Biographical Digression: Philip Ginder

THE STORY ABOUT THE SETTLEMENT of the Panther Valley and its development into a major industrial center is a story about people.

Before 1750 Immigrants pouring into the port of Philadelphia had taken up the best farming land south of the Blue Mountain, so Ginder, like Weiss, had to cross over the Blue Mountain to find suitable land.

When Ginder built his mill and settled along the Mahoning Creek several miles west of the Weiss settlement is not definitively known. However, in late 1786 Ginder obtained a warrant for a piece of land

Artist's conception Philip Ginder discovering coal in 1791 on Sharp Mountain near present-day Summit Hill

situate on the Northwest Branch of the Mahoning Creek in Penn Township, Northampton County containing three hundred and eight acres one hundred & fifty-three perches & the allowance of six p. cent.[3]

According to Korson by 1791 Ginder had built his own water-powered gristmill and was well into the milling business.[4] It is highly likely that some of the output of his mill was sent downstream on the rafts of Jacob Weiss. Settlers in this part of the country fed their families by the produce grown on their own farms, as well as by the hunt. So, it is not a stretch of the imagination to believe that

2

Ginder hiked over the surrounding countryside with an eye for the game that the sparsely settled area provided.

According to a historical paper penned by Dr. Thomas C. James and later presented to the Historical Society of Pennsylvania, in a story that is now one of the prevailing legends in the Southern Pennsylvania Anthracite field, while hunting on Sharp Mountain sometime in 1791, Ginder stumbled upon some black stones that would later turn out to be anthracite. Suspecting the black rocks he had found were stone coal, Ginder presented them to Jacob Weiss, who sent them off to important relatives and acquaintances back in Philadelphia. The rocks turned out to indeed be stone coal, of rather high quality, and the rest is, as they say, history.

Further historical research has revealed that Jacob Weiss already knew about stone coal, having, a few years earlier, discovered coal outcrops along Room Run, a small stream that had its headwaters in the same hills as the Panther Creek. According to Christopher Baer, the Jacob Weiss papers reveal that an unknown "hunter" was hired by Weiss to be on the "lookout" for these black rocks. Weiss sent the coal samples from the Room Run outcrops to his Philadelphia contacts, but the samples proved to be of poor quality and difficult to burn.[5] It was not until 1830 that the outcrops exposed along Room Run would be re-discovered by the LC&N, resulting in the laying out of the village of Nesquehoning and the construction of the Room Run Railroad.

According to Korson, before taking the stones to Weiss, Ginder verified, in the forge of a nearby neighbor, that the rocks he found would indeed burn. The coal turned out to be of such a high quality that within a year the Lehigh Coal Mine Company (hereinafter LCMC), a joint stock company, was formed in Philadelphia to exploit this discovery.

Lumbering in Panther Creek Valley

MANY INFLUENTIAL MEN were involved in the formation of the LCMC. One of these was John Schropp, another Bethlehem Moravian, who served as the city's Warden from 1790 until his death in 1805.[6] Schropp was also a manager and stockholder of the LCMC, involved in some of the on-the-site operations of the company, including the construction of a road from the Lehigh River at the mouth of the Nesquehoning Creek, to Hell Kitchen Run, near the Room Run outcrops. As a result, Schropp was very familiar with the area drained by the Panther Creek Valley.[7]

Unlike today, at the time of Ginder's coal discovery, the Panther Creek Valley was overgrown by a thick hemlock forest. In 1791 Schropp petitioned the Pennsylvania Legislature for permission to construct a bridge over the Lehigh River, at Bethlehem, with plans to use wood from trees felled in the forests of the Panther Creek. On April 3, 1792, Pennsylvania's first Governor signed an act authorizing Schropp to build this bridge.

After contracts had been let, Hemlock trees along the Panther Creek were harvested. Although a road from the Room Run outcrops to the Lehigh River was not made until 1803, the closest route from the Panther Creek to the Lehigh River followed a Native American trail through the Room Run gap in Locust Mountain to the mouth of the Nesquehoning Creek on the Lehigh.

It is this author's belief that the trees felled along the Panther Creek, were cut to useable sizes at the Union Sawmill, located at the mouth of the Nesquehoning Creek and entered the Lehigh River there. Timber was then floated down the Lehigh and drawn ashore near the Bethlehem Ferry. An uncovered bridge over the Lehigh River, was completed on September 27, 1794, and opened the following day.[8]

Early Mining Failures

THE LCMC MADE EARLY ATTEMPTS to mine coal at the Sharp Mountain site. While these attempts enjoyed some limited success, at that time there was no established market for anthracite and the route from mine to market was completely undeveloped. The men did, however, conduct searches for coal in the area, and purchased significant amounts of land in the Panther Creek and Room Run valleys, amounting, by 1798 to 8,665 acres.[9]

"Coal Benches Locust Mt Opposite Lehigh Summit Mines" Henry Darwin Rogers, *The Geology of Pennsylvania*, 1858 II, 1008

After a few years of trying to manage and exploit the property from Philadelphia, the managers of the LCMC resorted to leasing their coal property. The earliest of the lessees was Jacob Cist, himself a stockholder in the LCMC, and the nephew of Jacob Weiss, for whom he was named. Cist and Company signed a 10-year lease of the LCMC on December 10, 1813, just in time to exploit a fuel shortage caused by the British blockage of the port of Philadelphia in the war of 1812. Cist hired a good friend, Isaac Abel Chapman, to be his man in the field, digging coal at the Sharp Mountain and Room Run sites, building coal arks at the Village of Lausanne at the mouth of Nesquehoning Creek, even rafting coal downstream to market. A man of many skills, Chapman was also a skilled surveyor and map-maker and extensively explored the entire area in 1817 and 1818. A pencil sketch in the Jacob Cist collection of the Luzerne County Historical Society showing coal outcrops on Locust Mountain, the northern

Jacob Cist (1782 – 1825)
Luzerne County Historical Society

4

boundary for the Panther Creek Valley, was likely Chapman's handiwork, and clearly implies that the valley was underlaid with coal seams.

While Cist and Company enjoyed some success in mining coal at Sharp Mountain and getting the product to market, there was still not enough consumer demand, nor financial capital to ensure significant profitability following the removal of the British blockade at the end of the war.

Another group of men, hot on the heels of Cist and Company, would bring enough financial capital and energetic determination to change the course of Panther Valley and American history.

[Left] Isaac Abel Chapman (1787-1827). Luzerne County Historical Society.

Josiah White and Company

MUCH HAS ALREADY been written about Josiah White and the events which brought him and his associates, Erskine Hazard and George F.A. Hauto to the Panther Creek region, including Korson's *Black Rock*. These events will not be recounted here. It is sufficient to state that Josiah White visited the Lehigh Coal region in December of 1817 and went back home to Philadelphia convinced that his calling lay along the Lehigh. The efforts of these men resulted in the formation of one of the oldest and longest-lived corporations in the United States, the Lehigh Coal and Navigation Company (hereinafter LC&N).

Josiah White (1781-1850)

Erskine Hazard (1790-1865)

White and company made their own lease of the LCMC coal lands in early 1818 and immediately set about increasing the size of the quarry that had developed at the site of Ginder's discovery.

LC&N Early Timeline

➢ 1818: Village of Mauch Chunk laid out at mouth of MC Creek.
➢ 1819: Completion of Stone Turnpike from Summit quarry to Mauch Chunk.
➢ 1827: Stone Turnpike replaced with gravity railroad.
➢ 1828: Summit Quarry opened just east of original quarry at Summit Hill.
➢ 1829: Completion of Lehigh Canal.
➢ 1838: Gravity Railroad extended into Summit Quarry.
➢ January 1841: Great flood of Lehigh River almost bankrupts LC&N.
➢ Spring 1846: Completion of return track for gravity railroad.

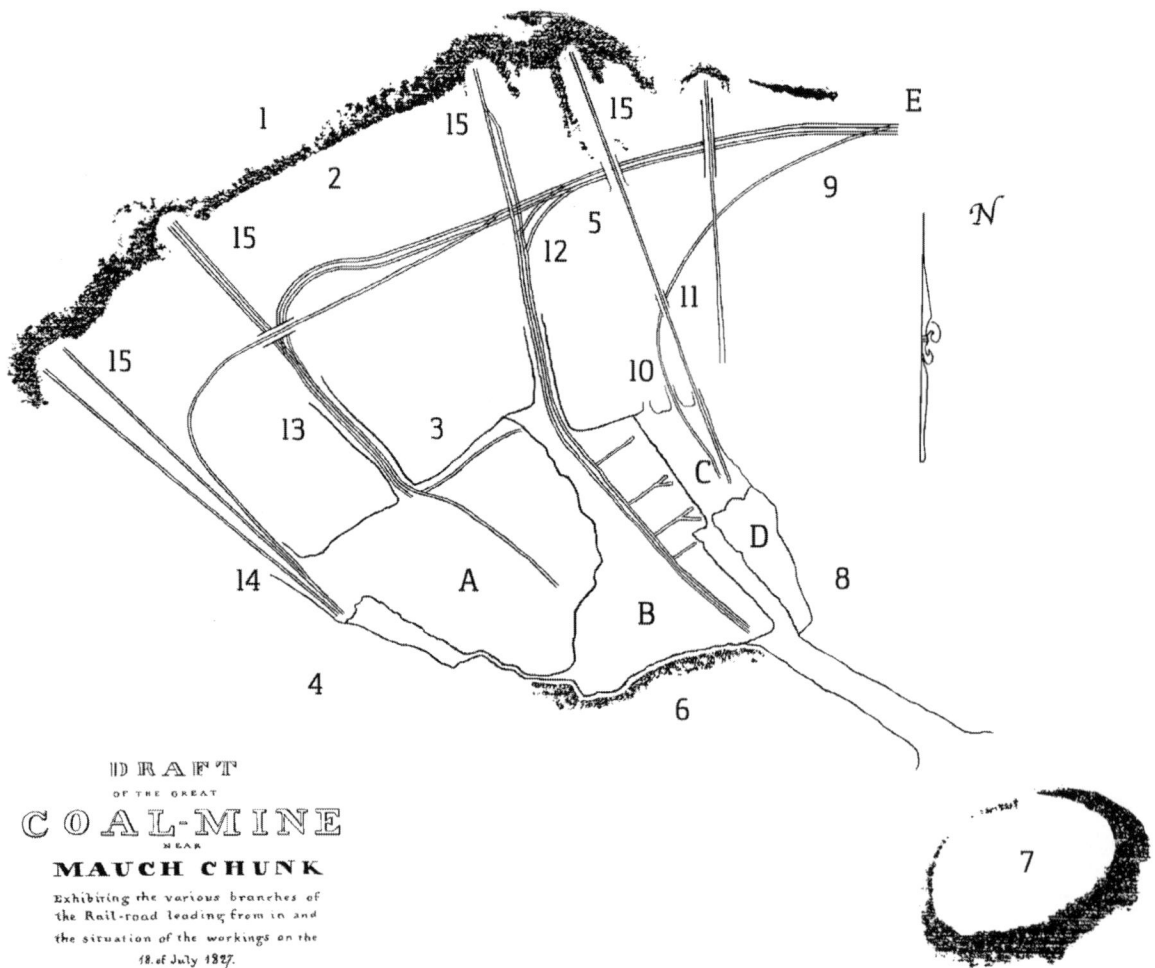

DRAFT
OF THE GREAT
COAL-MINE
NEAR
MAUCH CHUNK
Exhibiting the various branches of
the Rail-road leading from in and
the situation of the workings on the
18. of July 1827.
I A Chapman

Isaac Abel Chapman's map of the "Great Quarry" at the summit of Sharp Mountain near present-day Summit hill, after the gravity railroad was in operation. In addition to a career as a surveyor, Chapman was an accomplished map-maker. Chapman surveyed the route of the railroad in the summer of 1826 and died in December of 1827. Special Collections, Lehigh University, Beyond Steel Item 2596. Adapted by the author from a map microfilmed image of the map, Hagley Museum

Legend

DRAFT of the Great Coal Mine Near Mauch Chunk Exhibiting the various branches of the Rail-road leading from it and the situation of the workings on the 18 of July 1827
I.A. Chapman

1. A mound of loose earth and decomposed coal, which originally covered the mine from which it has been removed
2. SPOIL BANK formed of earth which covered the coal
3. High bank containing a Stratum of Sand Stone called the "North Fort"
4. On this side of the main opening the coal is covered in a similar manner to that on the East side and extends to an unknown distance.
5. To this intersection all the road lines (except N"L) descend, and here the horses are attached to the waggons to haul them to the summit at Slush hill whence they descend by gravity to Mauch Chunk.
6. The different benches of the mine were measured along the direction of the dotted line F.M. and were found as follows viz:
   - Bench D. at F is the upper surface of the coal when uncovered
   - Bench C C C at G is 16 feet below F
   - Bench B at H is 15 feet below G. The mine then gradually descends to L.
   - Bench A on floor of the mine is 18 feet below L. The descent is the gradual from K to L.
   - Bench marked N at M is 39 feet above L.
7. On this side is a narrow sandstone, forming the boundary of the present opening, called the "South Fort".
   From this line the ground gradually descends to the North & to the South.
8. Spoil Bank. Composed of loose earth which formerly covered the mine whence it has been removed.
9. On this side of the main opening the coal is covered with earth, varying in thickness from _____ to _____ feet. Its depth and extent are unknown.
10. This line descends to the first intersection at E
11. First Entrance No. 1
12. Second Entrance No. 2
13. Third Entrance No. 3
14. Fourth Entrance No. 4
15. Uncovering Lines
A. This part of the mine forms the bottom or floor of the present workings.
B. This bench is about 15 to twelve feet above the bottom floor marked A.
C. This bench is about 16 feet above the bench marked B.
D. This bench is about 10 feet above the bench marked C C C
E. Main Line of Railroad to Mauch Chunk

The Stone Turnpike

IN THE FALL OF 1818, after establishing the village of Mauch Chunk at the mouth of the Mauch Chunk Creek, White and company began surveying a road from the mine to the Lehigh River, nine miles distant. White foresaw a railroad eventually laid over his new road, and so built the road such that it was continuously descending-with no undulation. White called this "the principle of never rising."

The turnpike was constructed, according to Elizabeth Morton, "during bitter winter months," and was completed early in 1819, although stoning of the surface would not be finished until 1822. During this time the company also successfully completed a descending-only navigation of the Lehigh and Delaware rivers.

In 1820, under the supervision of an early LC&N employee named James Broderick, the LC&N quarried and sent down the Lehigh River the unprecedented quantity of 365 tons of Sharp Mountain coal. This saturated the market, but impressed Philadelphia consumers who previously hesitated to convert from wood to anthracite.

The next year Broderick moved with his wife to a location near the site of the quarry, the first family to do so. Around them the small village of Anthracite, later Summit Hill, would grow. Broderick would later join other men in forming their own individual enterprises, to take contracts with the LC&N.[10]

The Gravity Railroad

THE STONE TURNPIKE was a tremendous improvement over the rough road previously laid down by the LCMC. And, while the cost of transportation had been reduced, from approximately $4.00 per ton to about 70 to 80 cents for the hauling from mine to river, the trip still took one day per load. This would stand in the way of any substantial increase in coal production.

Josiah White's solution to the problem was a railroad. White began construction of the Summit Hill to Mauch Chunk gravity railroad in early January 1827 and had it completed by May of that year.

Within a few years the descending only navigation was replaced by the Lehigh Canal, a slackwater navigation system of the Lehigh River that allowed both descending and ascending traffic. One of the engineers hired by White and Hazard to construct the Lehigh Canal, was the renowned Canvass White, of Erie Canal fame. Before his death Canvass White, (no relation to Josiah,) would not only seed the Lehigh Coal region with his handiwork, but also his progeny.

The Return Track

THE MAUCH CHUNK RAILROAD operated as a single-track carrying coal from the Sharp Mountain quarry from 1827 to the end of the 1845 season. During that period the railroad carried more than 1.7 million tons of coal.[11] The idea of a return track to the mines was first considered in 1829 but shelved soon after because the demand for coal was not sufficient to justify the expense. Company finances would soon change that. In 1844 the need for a return track was

Engraved portrait of Canvass White, as published in *Lives and Works of Civil and Military Engineers of America*, by Charles B. Stuart

born out of urgent economic necessity. As happened many times during its history, the LC&N was facing certain financial "embarrassment," if not utter ruin.

Expanding Coal Production

AT THE BEGINNING of the 1840s, mounting debts and interest payments had forced the LC&N to suspend the payment of dividends, and the price of coal was on a steady decline.

In early January 1841, the LC&N Managers held a regularly scheduled Stockholders' Meeting. The managers had prepared their usual Report, which, although commenting on the problematic situation, looked confidently to the future. Events proved this confidence unjustified.

Winter ice jams in the Lehigh and Delaware rivers were a common occurrence. From a stereopticon slide "Ice-Gorge in the Delaware River, Port Jervis, N.Y., 27 Feb 1875."

Historian Paul Johnson has said that Mother Nature intervenes whenever humans build houses of straw, or paper. The day before the stockholder's meeting a winter thaw and rainstorm sent a tremendous mass of ice and water rushing down the Lehigh River. The *Mauch Chunk Courier* noted:

> About 11 o'clock in the evening, the water in the Lehigh having rose several feet above any former freshet within the recollection of our oldest inhabitants . . . the guard bank attached to the first dam above this place gave way, and the mighty waters came down with the most tremendous and awful destruction.[12]

This flood, striking at the most inopportune moment, destroyed the company's only source of income, the navigation, with the result that appeals for loans to repair the works were completely unsuccessful. While the Company could still mine coal and get it to the Lehigh River there was no way to get the coal to paying markets.

Unable to borrow in the money market, the company mortgaged all its property.[13] Interest payments on this loan further increased the Company's money outflow and required even greater income. However, there was some good news. By July 12 of 1841 boats were being loaded with coal at the Mauch Chunk schutes and would soon travel down the repaired navigation.[14]

If the price of coal had not continued its steady decline, things might have been fine. But intense competition among the various coalfields, starting in 1841, dropped the price of white-ash lump coal to $3.25 a ton in 1843. The price, which had peaked at $6.72 in 1837, would remain below $4.00 a ton until 1854.[15] By 1843 the revenue of the LC&N had dropped so much,

Carbon County Gazette, **17 Jul 1844, Dimmick Memorial Library (DML)**

that the LC&N completely suspended interest payments on its old loans, and paid interest on the new mortgage loan with coal, instead of cash.[16]

Josiah White understood that the solution to the problem was to increase income by expanding coal production and sales. However, traffic on the original descending gravity railroad had reached its maximum capacity. Increasing coal production could only be accomplished by constructing a return track and expanding coal mining into the Panther Creek Valley, located just north of the original quarry. In June 1844 the LC&N Board of Managers unanimously adopted Josiah White's plan.

The "Coal Mne" at Summit Hill." Benjamin Silliman, a geology professor from Yale, visited the Mauch Chunk coal regions in May of 1830. He reported that the Great Quarry on Sharp Mountain, had "much the appearance of a vast fort, of which the central area is the parade ground and the upper escarpment is the platform for the cannon." This sketch, first published in the January 1831 issue of *Silliman's American Journal of Arts and Sciences*, shows that his description is fitting. Richard Richardson, *Memoir of Josiah White*, Philadelphia, 1873, 48.

Coal in the Panther Creek Valley

THE SUMMIT OF SHARP MOUNTAIN was a unique location where the mammoth vein, the motherlode of the anthracite coal seams in Pennsylvania, was located on top of the mountain covered by only a thin layer of dirt. In 1828 the Company discovered another section of the mammoth vein slightly southeast of the original quarry and near the miner's village, where the coal cars were hauled by mules for their descent by gravity to Mauch Chunk. Here coal could be quarried as in the old mine. The great significance of this find was that from this point the loaded cars could descend directly to Mauch Chunk, without having to be hauled by mules to the summit. This discovery, although not as extensive as the original quarry, was immediately exploited, and became known as the Summit Mines. Here Slope No. 1 was driven down the dip of the coal vein and worked until 1859, when the mines caught fire, and became Summit Hill's famous burning mine. Following the discovery and exploitation of this new quarry, the old quarry became simply known as the "Old Mines."

"East Workings in Old Lehigh Summit Mine." In 1828 the LC&N discovered another major outcrop of the mammoth coal vein on Sharp Mountain, just southeast of the Great Quarry. Mining began at this location, known as the "Summit Mines" and later as the "Propellor Mines" and in 1838 the Company extended the gravity railroad into the quarry. The immense depth of this quarry required the used of inclined planes. Here Josiah White experimented with powered inclines, first using animal power and later steam engines. His findings assisted with his later design for the Backtrack, which required steam powered inclines at Mount Jefferson and Mount Pisgah. Henry Darwin Rogers, *The Geology of Pennsylvania* II, 66

The LC&N would have been quite content to continue quarrying coal forever on top of Sharp Mountain had the Old Mines been, as they had been frequently described, "entirely inexhaustible." But the description proved to be wishful thinking, and in 1847 the quarry finally gave out and the newer Summit Mines proved very difficult to keep free of water. By then the LC&N had already expanded into the Panther Creek Valley, which lay to the north of the quarry, and encompassed even greater quantities of coal.

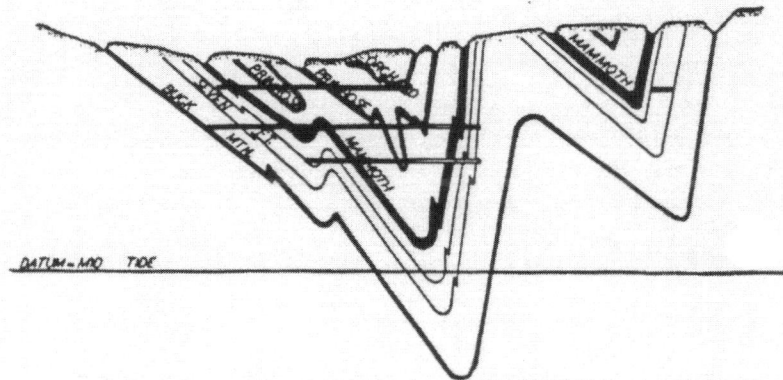

SECTION 2600' EAST OF NESQUEHONING TUNNEL

Cross-section through coal seams in the Panther Creek Valley east of Room Run. Michael Shegda, History of the Lehigh Coal and Navigation Company to 1840, unpublished Ph.D. dissertation, Temple University, 1952.

This coal would also prove rather difficult to extract, due to the veins being pitched at extreme angles, and also due to the veins being located deep underground.

11

It is not known definitively when coal was first discovered down in the Panther Creek Valley, or who made the discovery. However, the Jacob Cist Collection of the Luzerne County Historical Society contains an undated sketch of the geological formation on Sharp Mountain, where Ginder made his discovery. The sketch depicts the coal vein at the Great Mine, as well as coal outcrops on Locust Mountain on the valley's northern boundary. By examining the sketch even inexperienced persons could have deduced that the veins outcropping on Sharp and Locust Mountains passed beneath the valley, and thus could be tapped.[17]

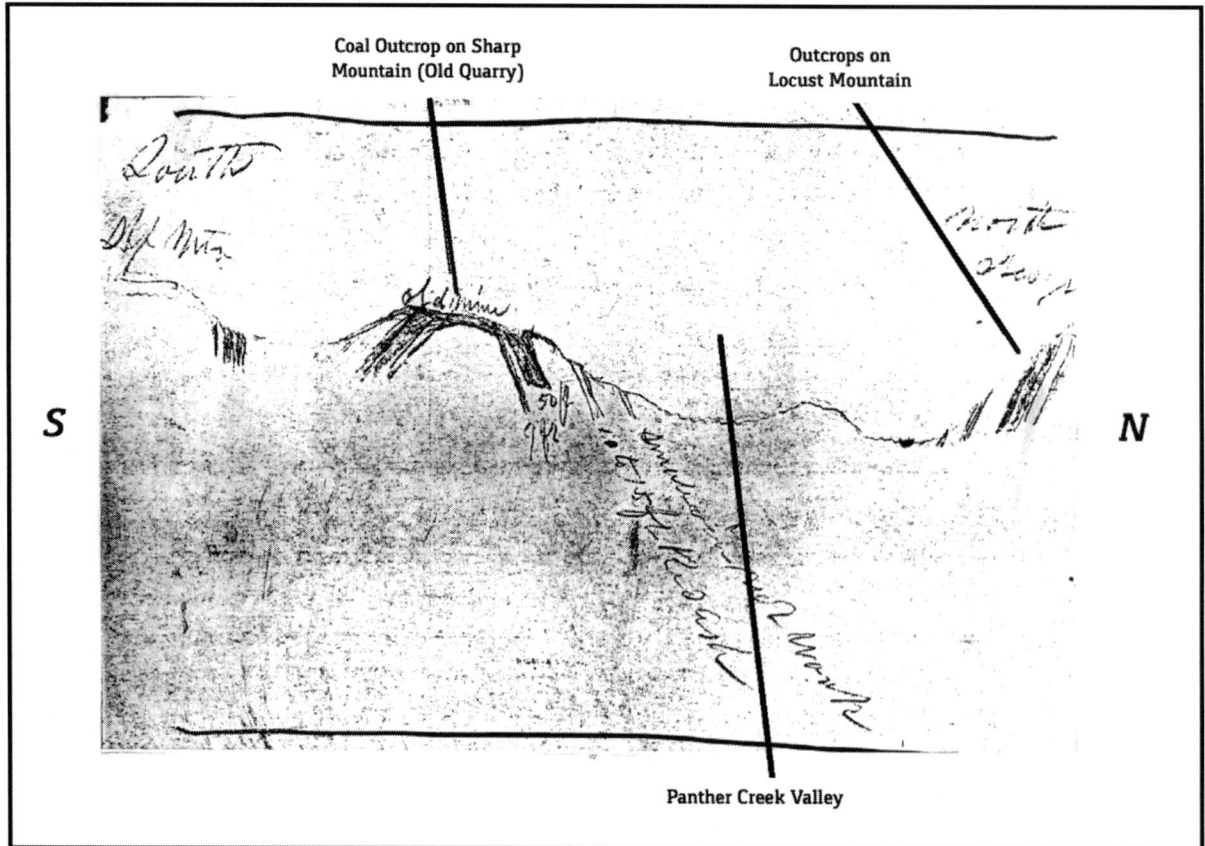

The earliest knowledge that the coal seam comprising the "Great Quarry" at Summit Hill also out-cropped on Locust Mountain, the northern boundary of the Panther Valley, was recorded in this drawing credited to Jacob Cist. The existence of these outcrops on the northern boundary of the Panther Valley implied that the coal veins passed under the Valley floor. This view is looking at the valley, toward the west, with Sharp Mountain to the south and Locust Mountain to the north. Jacob Cist, "Sketch of Lehigh Coal Mine," Luzerne County Historical Society

By January of 1830 Josiah White, who had been in contact with both Jacob Cist and Isaac Chapman, comprehended the extent of the coal veins that lay in the triangle of land owned by the LC&N. In the Company's Annual Report for 1829, Josiah White confidently stated:

. . . when our successors have done quarrying, they may follow the vens under ground eastward to the river about seven miles more, and five miles in a western direction.[18]

A Questionable Story

ACCORDING TO ONE doubtful account, Jacob Horn was the LC&N employee who discovered coal in the Panther Valley. In this account, the LC&N originally assigned Horn to Sharp Mountain in the area between Mauch Chunk and the Old Quarry. But Horn insisted that they were looking in the wrong place. Finally, after two winters of fruitless searching, Horn was told to "take his own head for

12

it" and with his gang of men, crossed over the range into the Panther Valley and located coal veins in the east end of the Valley. Tunnel No. 5 and Slope No. 4 eventually tapped these veins.[19]

This story is problematic. Born in 1816, Jacob Horn's parents didn't move to Mauch Chunk until 1825. By then, the LC&N had explored most of Sharp Mountain and knew the extent of the coal veins. Additionally, there is no evidence that coal veins ever outcropped near the valley floor.

There are other claims as to the first discoverers of stone coal in the Panther Valley, the Moser family.

Early Settlers in the Panther Creek Valley: The Moser Family

John Moser (1805-1893)
Lansford *Valley Gazette*, Sep 1976, 12

ALTHOUGH THE EXPANSION of coal mining into the Panther Creek Valley came from the southern direction, immigration of Caucasian settlers into the valley started from Tamaqua at the western end. Burkhart (aka Burkhard) Moser and his wife are generally acknowledged to be the first settlers in Tamaqua, located at the western end of the Valley, where the Panther Creek empties into the Little Schuylkill River. According to some sources, this occurred in 1799. Later, in 1817

(Berkhard) Moser discovered coal, which was successfully mined until 1874, when the breakers were burned and the mines ruined, at a loss of $1,500,000 to their owners.[20]

John Moser, the son of Burkhart Moser, moved eastward into the Panther Creek valley in 1827, building a cabin and settling at a location later named Coaldale. Some sources state that the Mosers were the first to discover anthracite coal in the Panther Valley. The Moser claim to coal mining tracts in the valley would later be challenged by the LC&N, resulting in long-running lawsuits.

Panther Valley Summary Timeline: Early 1840s

➤ LC&N plans to drive Panther Valley Tunnel No. 1, the "Bone Hollow" Tunnel.

LC&N Expansion Plans Move Forward

BY 1840 BEFORE LC&N FINANCES had reached the crisis stage, Josiah White had already turned his gaze northward to the Panther Creek Valley.

The mountains on each side (of the old mine), and forming the edges of the Coal Basin, are about 500 feet above the valley near to, and parallel with it. These mountains, extending about 13 miles in length, admit of drifts being run towards the bottom of all the veins in the Coal Basin, by which means the veins can be drained and worked by descending roads from the coal to the river. There is room for more than ten drifts, without interfering with each other. These drifts can be made at a moderate expense when needed, and produce more than 100,000 tons of coal each, per annum.[21]

Josiah White had always had a "hands-on" involvement with LC&N operations. He continued this as an Acting Manager following incorporation. After his retirement as Acting Manager in late 1831, White continued his involvement as a member of the Board of Managers Executive Committee. In this capacity he aggressively pushed expansion into the Panther Creek Valley even before work on the gravity railroad return track had started.

The "Bone Hollow" Tunnel

THE LC&N'S FIRST EFFORTS at mining in the Panther Valley began west of the Sharp Mountain quarry, where a stream of water sprang forth in a hillside hollow. This rivulet later supplied the reservoir for steam engines at the head of the

To Contractors.

PROPOSALS will be received at the office of The Lehigh Coal & Navigation Company either in Mauch Chunk or Philadelphia until the 7th of next month, for mining and delivering into boats from the summit hill mines 200,000 Tons of Coal, during next season. The Company propose to divide the mines, into two or more parts, and to be worked by as many companies of contractors. Specifications & mode of working the mines can be seen and blank proposals had at either of the above offices. For further information apply to the superintendent or mine agent at Mauch Chunk.

                        E. A. DOUGLAS,

Mauch Chunk,   }   Supt. & Eng.
Nov. 19th, 1844. }   30tl

Carbon County Gazette 21 Nov 1844, DML

Panther Creek inclined plane No. 2. Here the LC&N drove the first tunnel in the Panther Valley. Originally known as the "Bone Hollow" Tunnel, later it was known simply as Springvale. Many more tunnels would be driven within the valley.

As the Great Quarry neared exhaustion, the LC&N expanded coal mining into the Panther Creek Valley, which lay just to the north of the old mine. This sketch depicts one of the first tunnels, which was driven into the hillside directly below the old quarry. Henry D. Rogers, *The Geology of Pennsylvania*

At an October 1840 Mauch Chunk meeting, Josiah White and the Executive Committee specified that the tunnel was to be driven through the conglomerate rock, 8 feet wide at the bottom and 7 feet wide at the top, and 8 feet high "in the clear." The Company was to pay the contractors $7 a lineal yard for driving the tunnel and $2.50 a yard for the air "rises." The LC&N was responsible for all materials.[22]

The Springvale Tunnel was labeled Tunnel No. 1. There was also a Tunnel No. 1 at Room Run started about the same time. More commonly known as "Packer's Tunnel," this opening was begun sometime prior to August of 1843.[23] Which of the two tunnels was started first is uncertain. however, deep mining at Room Run had been going on since the early 1830s using drift mines, and the Hacklebernie Tunnel had been driven in the 1820s.

The LC&N awarded the contract to drive Panther Valley Tunnel No. 1 to "Captain" Alexander McLean and David Williams. Williams was supposedly the first Welshman to settle in the area and was influential in establishing the Welsh Congregational Church in the Valley. Beyond that, little is known about him.[24]

Not so with Alexander McLean.

Biographical Digression: Alexander McLean (1801-1868)

BORN IN IRELAND in 1801, by 1819 Alexander McLean had arrived in Mauch Chunk, a young man with energy to spare just as the LC&N was embarking on its ambitious program. McLean signed the LC&N's first transportation contract, to haul coal over the newly constructed stone turnpike.

McLean's parents disapproved of his emigration to America and refused financial support. His maternal grandfather, John Leslie however, stepped up, providing him with a hundred pounds sterling, with which he paid his travel expenses, and enough left over to purchase mules and wagons for his coal hauling enterprise.[25]

> These were primitive times, and Mr. McLean often told how he and his wagoners returning in the night upon their empty wagons from Mauch Chunk to the mines, a distance of about nine miles, would hear the howl of wolves and the cry of panthers near the wagon road, in the then almost unbroken wilderness.[26]

McLean continued to provide coal transportation from the Sharp Mountain mines to the Lehigh River following the completion of the gravity railroad, and took mining contracts at the summit, as well, with Alexander Lockhart.[27]

By early 1834 McLean had moved again, this time to the site of the Company's great quarry on Sharp Mountain, where he built his own house and dug his own well on LC&N property. In return, the LC&N gave him the use of the house "rent free" for five years. Alexander McLean also operated a tavern in Summit Hill, a village that developed near the site of the Old Mines.[28]

McLean's home, the largest one at this time on Sharp Mountain was big enough to board many of the miners who arrived at the summit without their families. McLean, a Presbyterian, was soon holding Sabbath meetings in his boarding house, where the men would gather to read the word of God and sing Psalms. This was the beginning of the Presbyterian church in that town.[29]

Alexander McLean entered business arrangements with other workers, which helped to spread financial risk. Besides contracting with David Williams to drive the Bone Hollow Tunnel, he entered mining contracts with Alexander Lockhart, the father of Mary Augusta Lockhart, who in 1872 would marry Asa Packer's youngest son Harry Eldred. McLean also partnered with George Kelso to drive Slope No. 1 in the early part of 1847. This slope was driven down along the south dip of the saddle shaped Mammoth vein just west of the Summit Mines, another quarry on Sharp Mountain.

In 1847 Alexander McLean completed the last of his contracts in the Panther Valley and retired from the business. By then, his son James had taken over his father's place in the Valley. Another son, Samuel, was the first man from Carbon County to be admitted to the Pennsylvania bar and was

To the Traveling Public.

THE SUBSCRIBER begs leave to inform the traveling public that persons will be carried between

Mauch Chunk and Philadelphia,

via Summit Hill, at the same rates as are charged by the other line; either by way of Pottsville or Port Clinton. The passengers leave C. Connor's hotel, Mauch Chunk, daily at 8 o'clock A. M., and arrive at Pottsville at 4 P. M.—take the cars on the Reading railroad the next morning after breakfast, (at 7, A. M.) and arrive at Philadelphia to dinner.

Returning—leave Pottsville daily at 11 A. M., arrive at Tamaqua in time to intersect the line of cars from Philadelphia, proceed to Summit Hill by coach, thence to Mauch Chunk, 8 miles, by railroad.

This being the old mail line, and believing the route to be the most pleasant and expeditious one, he hopes to receive a share of the traveling patronage.

Fare from Mauch Chunk to Philadelphia, $3 50.

ALEX. McCLEAN.

Summit Hill, Oct. 2, 1843.—28 4t

From the *Carbon County Transit*,
17 Oct 1843, DML

later elected Congressman from Montana.[30]

In 1848, Alexander McLean moved with his family to a farm on the Old Carey Town Road, in Wilkes-Barre, where he built "a fine house after the colonial fashion," and became a director of the First National Bank of Wilkes-Barre.[31]

Historic American Buildings Survey, Creator. Alexander McLean House, 156 Carey Avenue, Wilkes-Barre, Luzerne County, PA 1933. Documentation Compiled After. Photograph. Retrieved from the Library of Congress https://www.loc.gov/item/pa0561/.

Panther Valley Summary Timeline: 1843

➢ LC&N Managers request estimates for the following work:
  o for a railroad from Tunnel No. 1 to the summit of Sharp Mountain.
  o for Panther Creek Inclined Plane No. 1, and a railroad to the foot of the plane from Tunnel No. 1.
  o estimates for driving Tunnels No. 3 and No. 4.
➢ By Late 1843 the Springvale tunnel was driven the length of the Great Quarry

Descent Into the Valley

During 1843 the LC&N laid the early groundwork for construction projects in the Panther Valley by requesting estimates for various pieces of work from the different contracting companies. In August of 1843 the LC&N requested Lockhart & McLean to estimate the cost of grading a railroad from the mouth of the Bone Hollow Tunnel up the hillside to intersect the original Mauch Chunk gravity railroad near the Old Quarry.[32]

A month later the LC&N requested Company Superintendent and Engineer Edwin Douglas to survey another railroad, this one from the Bone Hollow Tunnel down the hillside to the foot of the proposed incline to the Summit of Sharp Mountain.[33] These sections of the railroad in the Panther Valley were completed by early 1845.

In December of 1843 Douglas was also requested to invite proposals for delivering cast iron rails for use inside the Bone Hollow Tunnel. Due to the Company's financial difficulties, payment for the rails ". . . to be made for the same in coal delivered at Mauch Chunk at $2 per ton." [34]

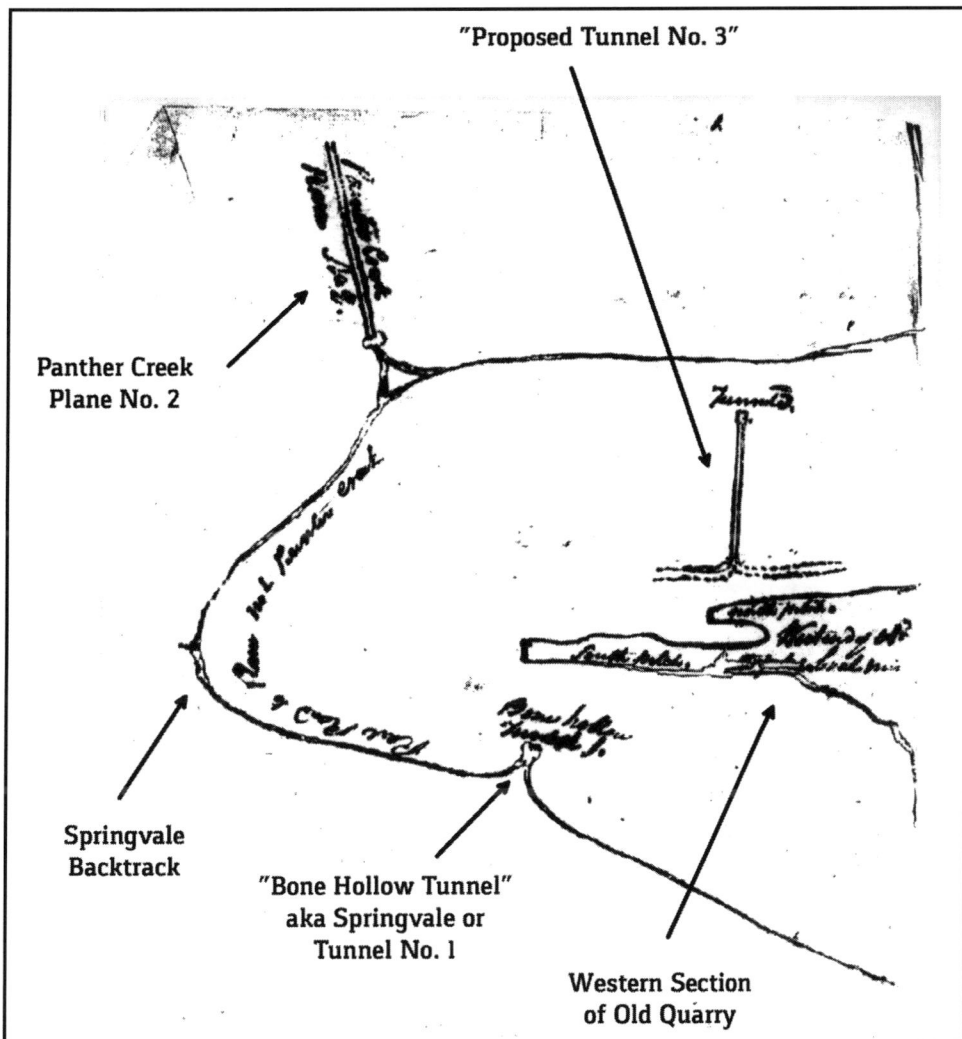

The surviving personal papers of Josiah White include this early undated sketch of first return backtrack into the Panther Creek Valley. The inclined plane at the upper left of the drawing was later known as Panther Creek Plane No. 2, or the Coaldale Plane. The tunnel in the right center of the sketch was later known as Tunnel No. 3, while the tunnel on the Backtrack was the "Bone Hollow Tunnel," later known as Tunnel No. 1, or the Springvale Tunnel. The leftmost portion of the great mine is shown extending between the two tunnels. Josiah White Papers, Norris Hansell Collection, National Canal Museum, a program of the Delaware & Lehigh National Heritage Corridor, Easton, PA

Panther Valley Summary Timeline: 1844

➤ Independent contractors enter arrangements to mine coal at the summit of Sharp Mountain.
➤ LC&N builds first mechanized coal breaker at Summit Hill.
➤ Coal struck and mined in Tunnel No. 1 (not shipped).
➤ Implementation of Josiah White's plan to separate Summit and Valley mines into different "districts" and award individual mining contracts.
➤ Contracts awarded for driving Tunnels No. 3 and No. 4. By year's end Tunnel No. 4 reached the Mammoth Vein.

Biographical Digression: Edwin A. Douglas (1804 - 1859)

EDWIN DOUGLAS was hired by LC&N co-founders Josiah White and Erskine Hazard in 1835 to serve as Chief Engineer during the construction of the Upper Division of the Lehigh Navigation. In 1844, Douglas was also appointed Company Superintendent, following the death by cholera of William H. Knowles.[35] Douglas designed and superintended construction of many LC&N projects in the Lehigh Valley, including the Ashley Planes of the Lehigh and Susquehanna Railroad (hereinafter L&SRR). Although the basic design for the Summit Hill and Mauch Chunk gravity railroad backtrack belonged to Josiah White, Douglas solved many of the practical challenges of the design, including problems with the safety or "barney" car. Douglas remained LC&N Superintendent and Engineer until his death in 1859, when John Leisenring, Jr. was chosen to fill his place.

Edwin Douglas, M.S. Henry,
History of the Lehigh Valley,
Easton, 1860, 385

Opportunity Knocks

THE LC&N SHIFT from hiring its own labor force to hiring contractors accelerated between 1828 and 1831, when, in October of that year, the LC&N let a mining contract at the Sharp Mountain quarry, opening the local mining industry to more individual entrepreneurs. The original contractors were ex-LC&N employees, men such as Samuel Holland and Samuel Barber, who were also contractors at the Room Run mines near Nesquehoning.

Around 1844 another group of men began to take contracts at the summit. This group included George Belford, Francis Weiss, Ira Cortright, John Leisenring Jr., and Richard Sharpe. Besides taking mining contracts at the summit, these men had other agreements amongst themselves. For example, while John Leisenring partnered with Ira Cortright for railroad construction in the Panther Valley, he partnered with Daniel Bertsch in the mining of coal. And Cortright and Bertsch, themselves,

18

partnered with other individuals. It is quite possible, since these men were all friends, that they formed arrangements on proposal making, contract acceptance and competition, or lack thereof. It is also quite possible that they also had labor sharing arrangements. How these arrangements worked as well as how profits were split is unknown.

Expansion into the Panther Creek valley also allowed Edwin Douglas and his proteges Robert H. Sayre, George W. Salkeld and Daniel Bertsch, Jr. to expand and develop their skills in railroad design and construction, particularly involving steam powered inclines. In contrast to the original descending railroad from the Summit to Mauch Chunk and the Backtrack, the Panther Creek design was in a perpetual state of flux as new mines were opened and as experiment and experience provided insight into better ways of doing things.

In 1844 the LC&N constructed a mechanized coal breaker at Summit Hill on the high point of the railroad before the gravity descent to Mauch Chunk. This early structure consisted of breaking, slating and screening machinery driven by a steam engine hauled over the mountains from Slope No. 1 at Room Run.[36] Later, following the construction of additional breakers within the valley, this breaker was nicknamed the "Old Crackers."[37] That same year Asa Packer and company installed a "coal cracker" at the Lehigh River coal landing for the Room Run mines.

"The Machinery for Breaking Coal." The Lehigh Coal and Navigation Company's first mechanized coal breaker was constructed in January of 1844 at the high point of the gravity railroad near the Summit Mines. Cylindrical grates and "crackers" are visible in the center of the sketch, directly below the overhead building. In the upper building, coal was broken by hand into two sizes. The larger sizes of coal fell down the incline leading to the right and down into a small shed overhanging the empty car. The smaller pieces fell directly down into the breaking machine, where the coal was again "fractured." It then fell through three separate screens or gratings, each with different sized holes and each inclined at a different angle. Breaker boys, also known as slate-pickers, manually accomplished the final separation of slate and other unusable material from the coal. "The Coal-Beds of Pennsylvania," *Illustrated News*, 15 Jan 1854, 36

"Breaking Coal by Hand and Grate." Although the Company's first mechanized coal breaker operated by steam power, laborers wielding sledgehammer and pickaxe manually cracked the larger lumps of coal, which were dumped onto grates as they arrived from the mines. After being cracked into smaller pieces by workers, the coal fell into the rotating cylindrical "crackers." "The Coal-Beds of Pennsylvania," *Illustrated News*, 15 Jan 1854, 36

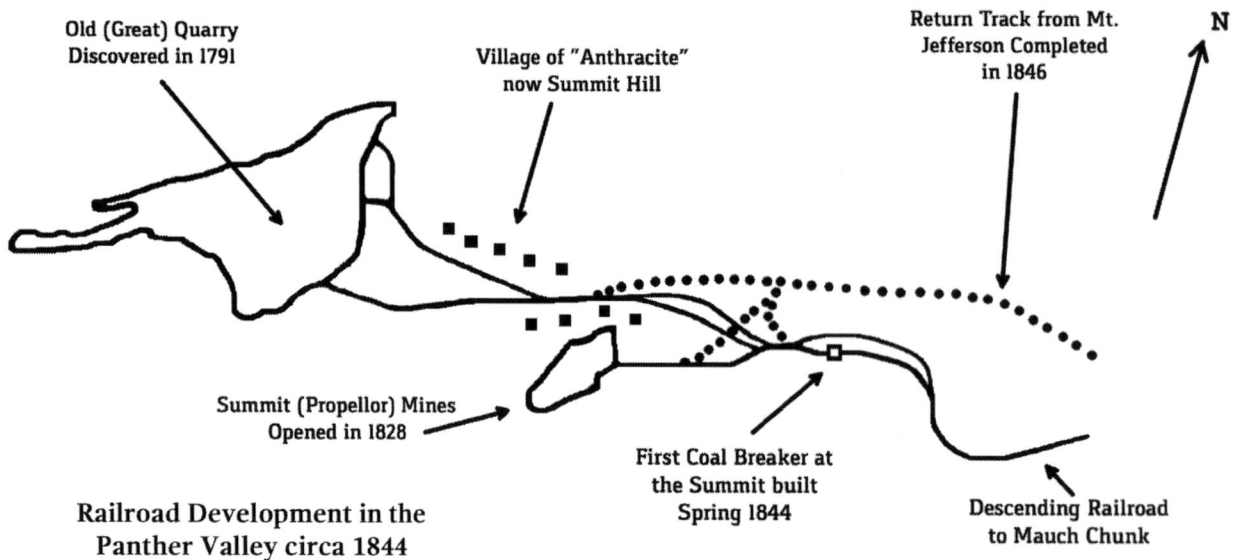

Old (Great) Quarry Discovered in 1791

Village of "Anthracite" now Summit Hill

Return Track from Mt. Jefferson Completed in 1846

N

Summit (Propellor) Mines Opened in 1828

First Coal Breaker at the Summit built Spring 1844

Descending Railroad to Mauch Chunk

Railroad Development in the Panther Valley circa 1844

Railroad Development at Summit Hill ca 1844. This schematic map details mining operations on Sharp Mountain and connection of the mines to the Mauch Chunk gravity railroad. In preparation for the expansion of coal mining from the Summit into the Panther Creek Valley, the LC&N constructed a mechanized breaker at the summit. Map adapted by the author from different sources.

The Bone Hollow Tunnel Strikes Coal

Since the Springvale Tunnel was driven underneath the Great Mine, it is not surprising that coal was struck as early as 1844 and mined throughout that season. Most likely this coal was simply piled at the tunnel mouth.[38]

In December of 1844, the LC&N let the contract for mining coal from the Springvale Tunnel to Alexander McLean and David Williams "at eighty cents for the larger coal and forty cents for the nut and chestnut."[39] McLean and Williams would continue to mine coal from the Springvale Tunnel until the end of 1847, when McLean retired from the business.

COAL DRIFT.

Burrowing Below the Great Mine, Tunnels 3 and 4

DIGGING JUST ONE TUNNEL in the Panther Valley was not part of Josiah White's plan. The opening of Tunnel No. 1 was soon followed by additional tunnels. Towards the end of 1843 the LC&N invited proposals for driving two tunnels southward into the hillside below the Sharp Mountain quarry, to attack the north dip of the Old Quarry's saddle-shaped vein, and to serve as a drain for the quarry. This was important, since keeping the pit free of water was becoming increasingly difficult.

Originally called "drift" mines by the company, these were true coal tunnels driven perpendicular to the thrust of the veins, penetrating the thick conglomerate rock that overlays and underlies all anthracite coal seams. These would be designated as Tunnels 3 and 4 and were to be the same size as the "Bone Hollow Tunnel" already in progress.[40]

Panther Valley coal mine Tunnel No. 3 as it appeared in the early twentieth century. This tunnel, driven by Daniel Bertsch and John Leisenring, extended south into Sharpe Mountain below the Old Quarry. Courtesy Dave Kuchta

Work on opening these tunnels began in early 1844. In January the contract for tunnel No. 3 was let to John Leisenring, Jr., and Daniel Bertsch. George Belford won the contract for tunnel No. 4.[41]

By January of 1845 one of these tunnels had passed through a vein of coal and the company anticipated that

> both are expected to reach, in the course of the present winter and coming spring, the principal strata forming the great mine.[42]

This "principal strata" was the Mammoth vein, the motherlode of all seams in the Pennsylvania anthracite region. Similar to the veins at Room Run, in the Panther Creek region this vein was folded back upon itself, sometimes reaching the incredible thickness of 50 to 100 feet. The second tunnel reached this "great vein" by May of 1846.[43]

This view of Panther Valley Tunnel No. 3 was taken by Summit Hill photographer C.H. Staudt, sometime in the late 1800s. Courtesy of the National Canal Museum, a program of the Delaware & Lehigh National Heritage Corridor, Easton, PA.

Biographical Digression: John Leisenring, Jr. (1818-1884)

JOHN LEISENRING JR, was a dynamic man reared in the family of a successful Mauch Chunk merchant, who was also one of the earliest landlords of Mauch Chunk's famous Mansion House Hotel. Leisenring Jr. quickly rose in the anthracite field to become very wealthy. After studying in the school of eccentric Irish schoolmaster "Jimmy" Nowlin, Leisenring entered the engineering ranks of the LC&N, under Edwin Douglas. While but a young man at 17 years of age, John was given responsibility for a complete section of the Upper Division of the Lehigh Canal, working with contractors George Law and Asa Packer. During the years 1837 and 1838 he worked on the

LC&N's railroad from White Haven to Wilkes-Barre.[44]

Too ambitious to remain simply an employee, Leisenring followed in the footsteps of other company men to go into business for himself. He left the LC&N sometime around 1844 to join a business firm operating on Sharp Mountain. Besides the contract with Daniel Bertsch to drive Tunnel No. 3, in August of 1844 these two men were awarded the contract to grade several sections of the return track of the Mauch Chunk gravity railroad.[45]

More than business connected Leisenring and Bertsch. On May 12, 1844, Leisenring married Caroline, daughter of Daniel and Catherine Bertsch.[46] John and Catherine made their home in Ashton, a small patch town in the Panther Valley, living there from 1844 to 1854.

Biographical Digression: Daniel Bertsch, Sr. (1801 - 1877)

BORN AT LOCKPORT, Pennsylvania, Daniel Bertsch was an early resident of Mauch Chunk, arriving in 1826. His first occupation was LC&N blacksmith, although he soon left the company to partner with Justus Gould, opening an independent blacksmith shop. Another ambitious man, in 1833 Bertsch built Mauch Chunk's Broadway House, one of the earliest hotels in Mauch Chunk that stood on the site of the present YMCA building on Broadway in Jim Thorpe.[47]

Bertsch expanded his reach into many areas, contracting to grade sections of the Beaver Meadow Railroad, and build dams and locks on the Lehigh Canal above Mauch Chunk. Bertsch also contracted to build segments of the Lehigh Valley Railroad (hereinafter LVRR) below Mauch Chunk, until his partner was killed by a premature powder blast. His son, Daniel Jr., later became the LC&N's Principal Assistant Engineer.[48] Bertsch, a veritable jack-of-all trades soon turned his attention toward the Panther Creek Valley and in January 1844, in partnership with John Leisenring, was awarded the contract to drive Tunnel No. 3. Later that year, the duo won a contract to grade Sections 8 & 9 of the LC&N's return track from Mauch Chunk to the mines. In December the LC&N awarded Bertsch and James Broderick the contract to mine 60,000 tons of coal from the southern half of the Old Quarry.[49]

Daniel Bertsch

The Panther Valley Switch-Back: Early Plans and Designs

CONCURRENT WITH THE DRIVING of the first three tunnels in the Panther Valley Edwin Douglas and his engineering crew prepared the initial designs for the Panther Valley railroad system. These early plans had the valley railroad divided into two sections, the first, the Springvale railroad and the second, the Panther Creek railroad. These divisions were soon consolidated and known simply as the Panther Creek Railroad, popularly called the Switch-Back section of the Mauch Chunk and Summit Hill Gravity Railroad.

This early work involved constructing an inclined plane leading west from the summit down to the mouth of Tunnel No. 1. The inclined plane was built to provide a means for lowering the tools and supplies needed in driving this tunnel and constructing attendant railroads. It may also have been used for hoisting coal from Tunnel No. 1 to the summit until Panther Creek plane No. 1 was placed into service. And, until 1848, when the temporary inclined plane was replaced by the Panther

Valley's first return backtrack, the Company used this plane for returning empties to the tunnel mouth.

Moncure Robinson. Author unknown [Public domain] via Wikimedia Commons

This inclined plane was short-lived, intended to be replaced by a gravity return leading from the summit to the valley floor similar in design to the original descending railroad. That is, constructed with wooden rails topped with lengths of strap iron.

The original design underwent many adaptations, including, at times, perhaps as many as six steam-powered inclined planes which pulled loaded cars to the summit of Sharp Mountain, where they were shunted onto the tracks heading for the Lehigh Canal at Mauch Chunk.

The LC&N's design for the exploitation of the coal in the Panther Creek Valley was a far cry from the original plans of Moncure Robinson, a railroad and canal engineer, who in 1829, advised the construction of a tunnel from the foot of Mount Jefferson on the southern side of Sharp Mountain into the Panther Creek valley.[50]

From hindsight such a tunnel would have simplified things, eliminating the need for the costly, complicated, and dangerous inclined planes. However, the use of a tunnel instead of the switch-backs, would also have made for a less romantic story. The gravity railroad would never have been given the name "Switch-Back" and the way history was preserved would have been entirely different. But Robinson's design was completely forgotten as construction of the Panther Creek section of the Mauch Chunk gravity railroad began.

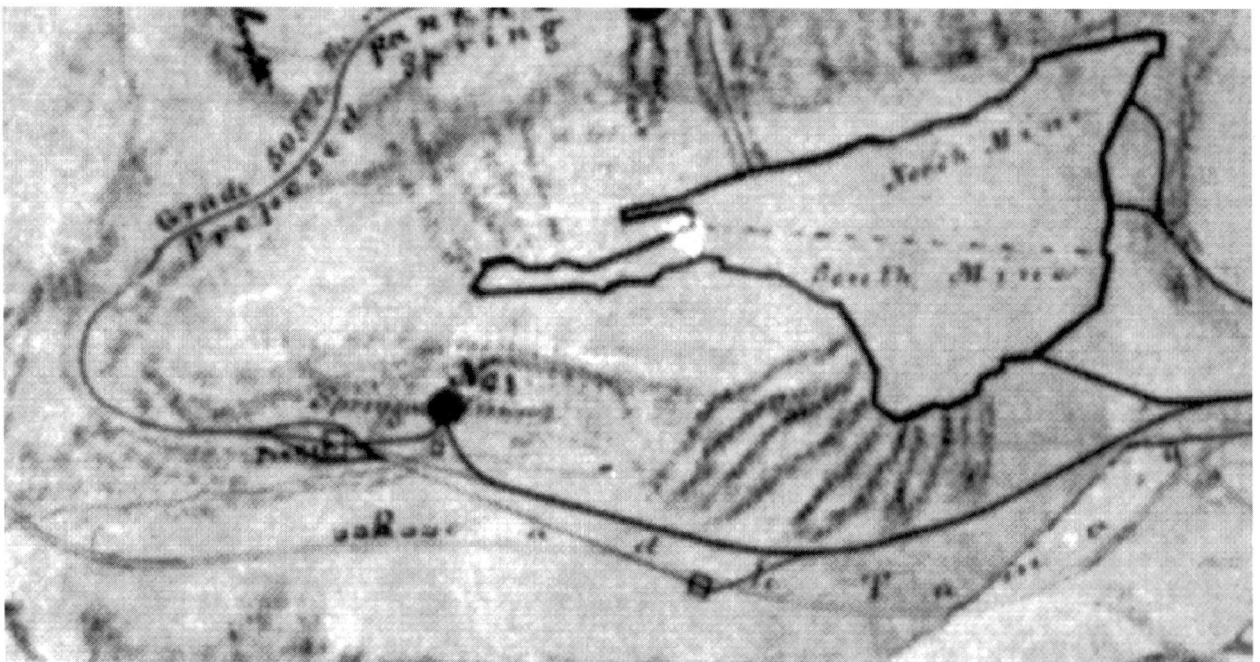

An enlargement of the 1845 LC&N Stockholder's map showing the first tunnel in the Panther Valley, Springvale, or Tunnel No. 1. An inclined plane leading from the summit was used for lowering supplies to the tunnel mouth, as well as hauling coal to the summit, prior to completion of Panther Valley Plane No. 1. Map adapted by author from John Hoffman 1845 LC&N Stockholder's Map

Biographical Digression: Moncure Robinson (1802-1891)

MONCURE ROBINSON, considered one of America's leading civil engineers as well as canal and railroad engineer, was locally noted for his involvement with the Little Schuylkill Railroad and the Philadelphia and Reading Railroad. He also performed many services for the LC&N including:

➢ Surveying the route for the Nescopeck Canal, to connect the Lehigh and Susquehanna rivers, one of several surveys made for a canal that would never be built. The two rivers were eventually connected by the LC&N's Lehigh and Susquehanna Railroad.

➢ Surveying the route and developing a plan for the return track of the Mauch Chunk gravity railroad. Robinson presented this plan to the LC&N Board of Managers in 1829, but it was shelved and superseded in 1845 by Josiah White's design.

➢ In 1830 the LC&N invited Moncure Robinson to survey the route for the Room Run Railroad, a task which he declined.

Panther Valley Summary Timeline: 1845

➢ At the January Stockholder's Meeting Josiah White presented his strategies for expanding coal production into Panther Valley.

➢ LC&N constructed a temporary inclined plane from Tunnel No. 1 to the summit of Sharp Mountain.

➢ Panther Valley Tunnel No. 3 struck the Mammoth Vein.

➢ LC&N lets contracts for grading Springvale Railroad to Tunnel No, 1 and Panther Creek Inclined Plane No.1.

➢ LC&N Board of Managers decides to build twenty houses at Tunnel No. 4, birthing the mining patch of Ashton.

➢ LC&N lets contracts for driving Tunnels No. 2 through 8, and railroads connecting these tunnels.

➢ LC&N continues mining at the Old Quarry and the newer Summit Mines.

Black Gold in the Panther Valley, Striking the Mammoth

JOSIAH WHITE's STRATEGY for the Panther Creek Valley was not presented to the LC&N stockholders until the Annual Stockholder's Meeting held in January of 1845. The presentation included a map previously surveyed, showing the proposed extent of operations in the Panther Creek Valley.

NOTICE
TO TUNNEL CONTRACTORS.

PROPOSALS will be received at the office of the Lehigh Coal and Navigation Company, Mauch Chunk, until the 12th of next month, for continuing the Spring-Vale Tunnel through into the Summit Coal Mines—a distance of about 900 yards. For further information, apply to
NATHAN PATTERSON, Mine agent.
E A. DOUGLAS sup't and engineer.
Mauch Chunk June 24th, 1845.

Carbon County Gazette, 24 Jun 1845, DML

In August of 1845 the *Carbon County Gazette* reported that mining contractor George Belford struck the Mammoth Vein in Tunnel No. 3 after driving through the conglomerate rock more than 600 feet

> and we have no doubt that in the course of two or three years more they will be able to mine and ship, annually, a million of tons.[51]

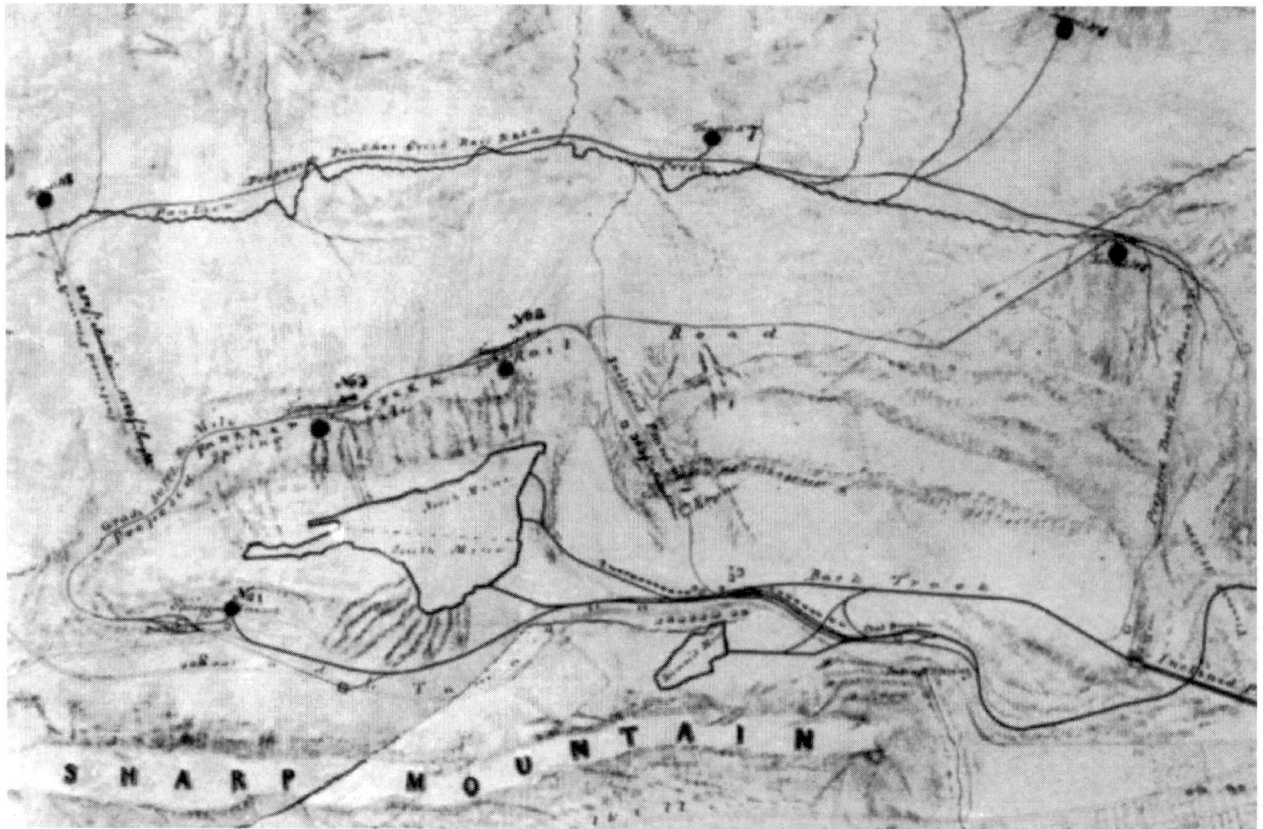

Closeup of Panther Creek coal region. A map of the original design of the Springvale and Panther Creek Railroads circa 1845. This map was prepared by Edwin A. Douglas and presented to the stockholders at one of the annual meetings. John N. Hoffman, *Anthracite in the Lehigh Valley of Pennsylvania 1820-45*, Washington, D.C., Smithsonian Institution Press, 1968, 108-109, Map of the Mount Pisgah Backtrack and Summit Rail Road, Line of the Proposed Panther Creek Railroad, January 1845

Work in Progress

ALTHOUGH THE RIGHT OF WAY had been surveyed by late 1843, Douglas wasn't authorized to advertise for proposals to grade the Springvale Railroad and construct inclined plane No. 1 until September of 1845.[52] Within two months, Douglas had let contracts for the work. Specifications included three coal storage pockets located near the mouth of Tunnel No. 1 and a railroad, leading past Tunnels No. 3 and 4 below the Great Quarry, to the foot of Panther Creek Plane No. 1. For purposes of contract allotment, the road was divided into three sections. The work was to be completed in 1846 and did not include a return track for letting down empties from the summit to the Springvale tunnel. This continued to be handled by the temporary Springvale inclined plane.

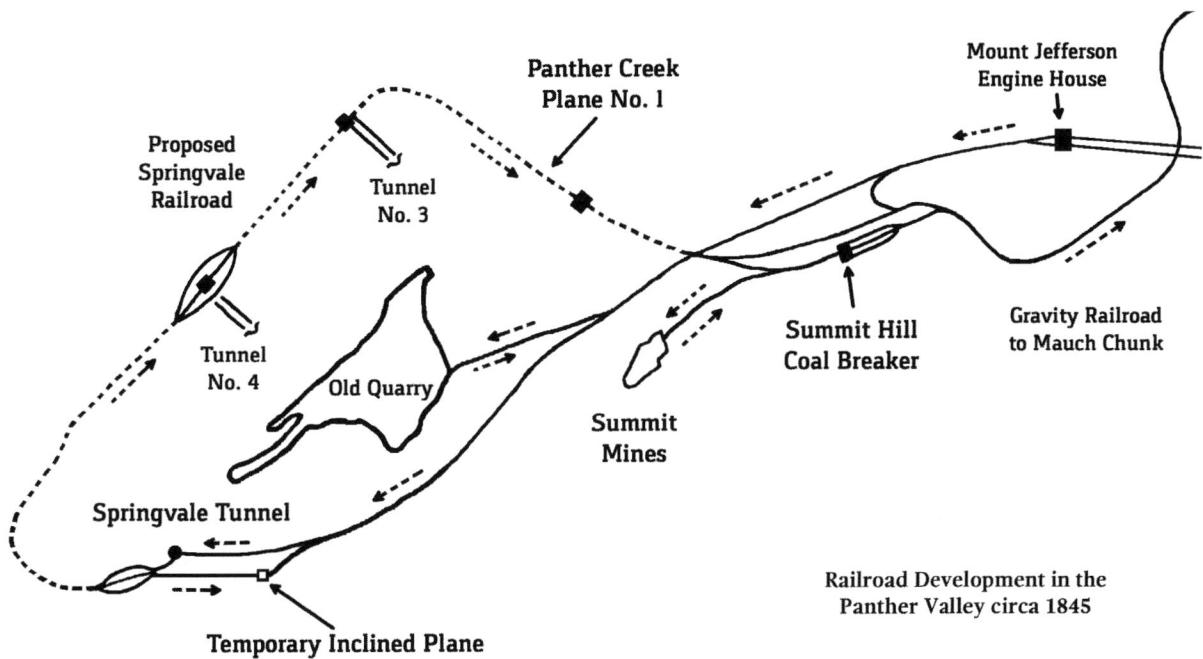

Railroad Development in the
Panther Valley circa 1845

Railroad Development in the Panther Valley circa 1845. Although a temporary inclined plane had been constructed from the summit down to Tunnel No. 1, and coal pockets planned for the tunnel mouth, Panther Valley Inclined Plane No. 1 was still in the planning stage, along with the railroad to the foot of this plane. Map created by author from various sources

Panther Valley Patch Towns

IN OCTOBER of 1845, recognizing the need for housing for the laborers flocking to the Panther Valley, the LC&N Executive Committee

> Resolved, that twenty houses to be built at Tunnel No. 4.[53]

These few houses, which the LC&N rented to the miners and contractors, were the birth of the patch town of Ashton, which would eventually, along with all the other valley mining patches at the east end of the valley, be incorporated into the Borough of Lansford. Although recognizing the need for housing in the Valley, it would be several more years before the LC&N began leasing lots in the Valley, and decades before the company would actually sell property.

More Mines

IN A SIGN that the LC&N was serious about development of the Valley mining operations, in October of 1845 the LC&N also requested proposals for mining coal, constructing railroad sections, and driving new tunnels, 200 to 300 yards long. Proposals were quickly received, and the following contract awards made:[54]

> ➤ Asa Lansford Foster & Robert Butler, grading Section 1 of the Springvale Railroad
> ➤ Sam Bedwell, constructing pocket No. 1 at Tunnel No. 1
> ➤ Ira Cortright and John Leisenring, grading Section 2 of the Springvale Railroad, and constructing Pocket No. 2 at Tunnel No. 1
> ➤ Francis Weiss and George Belford, grading Section 3 of the Springvale Railroad, and

27

constructing Pocket No. 3 at Tunnel No. 1
- ➤ Asa Lansford Foster and Robert Q. Butler, to drive tunnel No. 2
- ➤ John Leisenring Jr and a Mr. Nunemacher to drive tunnel No. 5
- ➤ George H. Davis to drive tunnel No. 6
- ➤ Thomas Broderick and a Mr. Ryan to drive Tunnel No. 7
- ➤ Samuel Spencer to drive tunnel No. 8. This fell through and the contract was awarded months later to Samuel Spencer and Cornelius Connor
- ➤ The Fatzinger and Salkeld Foundry in Mauch Chunk was awarded a contract to construct

> . . . four stationary steam engines one duplicate engine for each of the two inclined planes on the Mount Pisgah back track railroad, and two engines for the foot of inclined plane No. 1 Panther Creek.

In addition to the construction work, the LC&N awarded the following mining contracts in the Valley:[55]

- ➤ Alexander McLean and David Williams to mine coal from Tunnel No. 1
- ➤ Ira Cortright and John Leisenring to mine coal from Tunnel No. 3
- ➤ Daniel Bertsch to mine coal from Tunnel No.4.

During the 1845 season, while pushing forward with expansion into the Panther Creek Valley, the company continued to mine coal from operations at the summit, including the Old Quarry, as well as a new quarry known as the Summit Mine.

Biographical Digression: Asa Lansford Foster 1798-1868

ISAAC CHAPMAN introduced Asa Foster to the LC&N, bringing him to Mauch Chunk in 1827 to manage the Company's regional store, which Foster later bought outright with James Broderick. Foster was married to Louisa Trott Chapman, a niece of Isaac Chapman.[56]

In 1829 Foster began publishing the region's first newspaper, the *Lehigh Pioneer and Mauch Chunk Courier*.[57] Like Chapman, Foster had a keen knowledge of coal formations and was adept at locating deposits. Before moving to Mauch Chunk Foster, along with Chapman, located coal outcrops in Luzerne County, which he exploited after Chapman's death. In 1836 Foster helped organize the Buck Mountain Coal Company, and a year later, after dissolving his partnership with Broderick, moved to Rockport on the Lehigh River.   The first load of Buck Mountain coal floated down the Lehigh in the Fall of 1840. Foster and the Buck Mountain Coal Company were victims of the January Flood of 1841 which destroyed both the shipping port for the Coal Company and Foster's finances. He returned to Mauch Chunk in 1844 and soon after relocated to Ashton, in

Asa L. Foster, Henry,
History of the Lehigh Valley, 368

Office of the Lehigh Coal and Navigation Company, Mauch Chunk, Oct. 27, 1845.

TO MINE CONTRACTORS.

PROPOSALS will be received at this Office until the 6th day of November, inclusive, for mining and delivering on the stands, from The Lehigh Company's Coal mines at Summit Hill, 290,000 tons of coal, and from the old Tunnel, 10,000 tons during the boating season of 1846; also for transporting the same to the landing at Mauch Chunk and shipping it into boats.

Propositions for the above can be made for one, two, or three years; the amount of coal to be delivered the second and third years to be determined by the company.

Proposals will also be received for driving 5 Tunnels each to be from 200 to 300 lineal yards in length.

For further information and specifications, apply to the, undersigned, or to Nathan Patterson, the Company's mine Agent, at Summit Hill.

E. A. DOUGLAS, Supt. & Eng'r.

Ads like these in Mauch Chunk newspapers brought ambitious men into the Panther Valley. *Carbon County Gazette* 30 Oct 1845, DML

time to take advantage of the opportunities there. Besides taking contracts, he served as Daniel Bertsch's bookkeeper and financial manager from 1845 until 1855.[58]

In the election of 1852 for Pennsylvania State Congress, Asa Lansford Foster ran against the renowned Asa Packer, losing to Packer, 1267 to 640. Packer ran for the Democratic Party and Foster ran for the Whig Party.[59]

In 1876 when the Panther Valley patch towns of Ashton, Storm Hill and Richdale were consolidated, the borough was named Lansford in honor of Asa Lansford Foster.[60]

Following his death in 1868 Foster's remains were interred in the cemetery in Upper Mauch Chunk near those of Isaac Chapman and other family members.

Biographical Digression: Robert Q. Butler (1818-1894)

ROBERT Q. BUTLER'S early working career was as a salesman in Foster and Broderick's Mauch Chunk store. When Foster relocated to Rockport in 1838 Butler went with him, serving as Rockport's postmaster until 1844. Butler then relocated to the Panther Valley where, along with Asa Lansford Foster, he took an LC&N contract to grade Section No. 1 of the Springvale Railroad.[61]

At the same time the LC&N also awarded these men the contract to drive Tunnel No. 2 in the Panther Valley, later known as Foster's Tunnel. In 1864 Butler partnered with Thomas Long to mine coal at Tunnel No. 10.[62]

Following his efforts at mining in the Panther Valley, Butler relocated to Mauch Chunk where he became employed at public service. In 1889 he moved with his family to Kansas City, Missouri.[63]

Biographical Digression: Ira Cortright (1811-1870)

The Allotment.

The following is the allotment made by the Lehigh Company to contractors proposing for the Mines and Tunnels advertised to be let a few weeks since.

SUMMIT MINES.

1st Division.		Weiss and Belford.
2	do.	Needham and Salisbury.
3	do.	Daniel Bertsch.
4	do.	McLean & Williams.
5	do.	Cortright, Leisenring, & Sharp.
6	do.	Daniel Bertsch.
7	do.	(old Tunnel) Andrews & White.
Transportation, Lockhart & Barnes.		

TUNNELS.

No. 2		Foster, & Butler.
"	5	Leisenring & Nunamacker.
"	6	George H. Davis.
"	7	Broderick & Ryan.
"	8	Samuel Spencer.

This notice in a Mauch Chunk newspaper shows quite a few contractors mining coal in Summit Hill and Lansford. *Carbon County Gazette* 20 Nov 1845, DML

IRA CORTRIGHT was born in Luzerne County but moved to Mauch Chunk sometime prior to 1838. In 1845 he took his first contract with the LC&N, partnering with John Leisenring, Jr. to mine coal from Tunnel No. 3, a newly opened mine in the Panther Valley. These two men also partnered to grade a section of the Panther Creek Railroad and construct coal pockets on the Springvale Railroad. Cortright also partnered with other valley contractors to mine coal at the Summit. In December of 1849, Cortright moved to Ashton, leasing a lot from the LC&N, for 11 years at $1 per annum. In 1856 Cortright was awarded the contract to mine coal from Tunnel No. 8.

Cortright soon moved to Bethlehem, although he still held mining contracts in the Panther Valley. He was deeply involved in the repair of the lower Lehigh Navigation following the great flood of June 1862 and took and managed contracts for the construction of the Bethlehem Section of the LC&N's L&SRR from Mauch Chunk to Easton, directly responsible for the masonry for the bridge for this railroad across the Lehigh at Bethlehem.[64]

Biographical Digression: Francis Weiss (1819-1888)

FRANCIS WEISS was a grandson of Jacob Weiss, the man who exploited Philip Ginder's coal discovery with the formation of the LCMC. His working life began on a farm and attached sawmill until 1837 when he joined the LC&N. Under Edwin Douglas Weiss worked as a surveyor on the initial designs of the L&SRR, which at that early date was stretching over the mountains from White Haven to Wilkes-Barre. His skill led to his appointment as Deputy Surveyor of Carbon County after its formation in 1843.

Weiss saw the burgeoning opportunities in the Panther Valley and quickly took advantage, teaming up with George Belford in late 1844 take the LC&N's 1845 coal mining contract for the north side of the Old Quarry. In 1844 Francis Weiss also received a contract to grade a section of the return track of the Summit Hill and Mauch Chunk gravity railroad.[65]

Weiss remained a contractor in the Panther Valley until 1854, when he moved to Fillmore (later known as Eckley) as a partner at the Council Ridge Colliery. Weiss remained there several years, before retiring and moving to Bethlehem in 1870.[66]

Francis Weiss
Luzerne County Historical Society

Biographical Digression: George Belford (1802-1873)

GEORGE BELFORD, another of the LC&N's earliest employees, began his career as a carpenter, building canal boats for the company, and later dams and locks on the Lehigh Canal's Upper Division. He built the dam and lock at the mouth of Stony Creek, and later constructed the masonry for the original Mount Jefferson engine house on the Backtrack. In 1844 he began taking mining contracts at the Summit, "taking charge" of the old "Propellor Mines" and partnering with such men as John Leisenring, Jr. and Francis Weiss.[67] When he retired, Belford purchased several contiguous lots on Broadway in Mauch Chunk and built a home that is substantially the site of the current Dimmick Memorial Library.[68]

Biographical Digression: James Broderick (1793-1875)

OUR NARRATIVE HAS ALREADY encountered James Broderick (also spelled Broaderick and

Brodrick,) one of the earliest employees of the LC&N. Broderick and his wife moved from Summit Hill to Mauch Chunk in 1832 to partner with Asa Lansford Foster and Dr. Benjamin Rush McConnell in the mercantile business. The LC&N was divesting itself of its old Company Store, which Asa Foster had been managing since 1827. In 1833 the Company sold off all its stock in the establishment, at cost, and closed the operation, which was

NOTICE.

The partnership of the subscribers, trading under the firm of Foster & Broaderick, was dissolved by mutual consent and its own limitation on the 31st ult. The business will be continued by A. L. Foster, at the same place, who is duly authorised to settle the business of the late concern.

A. L. FOSTER,
JAMES BROADERICK

April 9, 1837.—17. 3t.

Mauch Chunk Coal Gazette, **24 Apr 1837, DML**

on the site of the present Carbon County Courthouse in Jim Thorpe. In June of 1833 the three men opened a new general store on the southwest corner of Broadway and Susquehanna Streets, across the street from the old Company Store.[69] In April of 1837 the business arrangement was dissolved, and the property was sold to Asa Packer, who would operate the "Corner Store" for several more decades. The site of the original Company store was donated for a courthouse following the formation of Carbon County in 1843.

Broderick left Mauch Chunk to return to Summit Hill to take more mining contracts. In partnership with Samuel Holland, Alexander Lockhart, James McLean, George Kelso and George H. Davis, he received an LC&N contract for 1837 to mine 160,000 to 180,000 tons of coal from the Old Quarry.[70]

In 1837 James Broderick temporarily retired to his farm in the Bloomingdale valley. Later, from 1855 to 1857, he leased the Buck Mountain mines. While engaged in this endeavor, he placed a locomotive on the Buck Mountain railroad named for Asa Lansford Foster.[71]

James Broderick continued to mine coal on contract from the old mine until it gave out. He then retired to his farm in the Bloomingdale valley. [72]

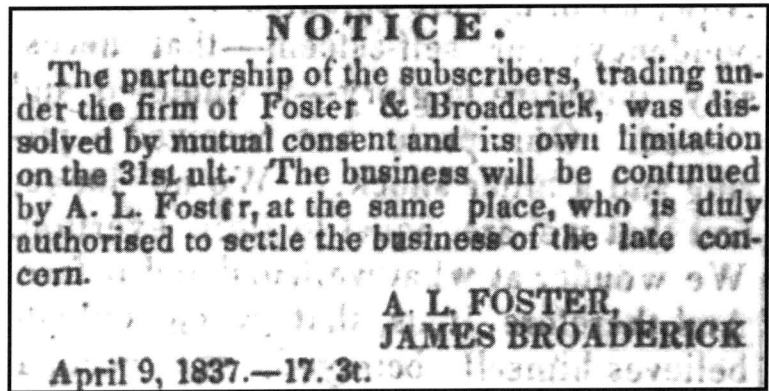

—Thomas Brodrick was re-elected Mayor of Wilkes-Barre on Tuesday by 450 majority. Mr. Brodrick is an old and well known citizen of this county and father of Mrs. T. F. Walter, of this place.—*Mauch Chunk Coal Gazette*

Biographical Digression: Thomas Broderick (1817 - 1886)

THOMAS BRODERICK was the son of LC&N contractor James Broderick, the man who supervised the mining of the LC&N's 1820 Lehigh River shipment of 365 tons of coal. When his father went into partnership with Asa Lansford Foster and Benjamin Rush McConnell to operate the store in Mauch Chunk, Thomas served as the firm's book-keeper. In 1837, after dissolving his Mauch Chunk partnership with Foster, James Broderick returned to Summit Hill to join a contracting firm consisting of Samuel Holland, Alexander Lockhart, James McLean, George H. Davis and George Kelso. Thomas went with his father, also in the capacity of book-keeper.

Thomas along with many of the famous of Mauch Chunk, was schooled by Jimmy Nolan, Mauch Chunk's notorious "Irish Schoolmaster." Thomas only remained in the Panther Valley for a short time. By 1849 he was living at Rockport, where he operated a store and where his wife died. He was involved with mining at the Buck Mountain mines until 1859, when he moved to the Wyoming Valley and was involved with coal mining in that region. He was elected mayor of Wilkes-Barre in 1880 and re-elected in 1883 and died in 1886.[73]

Biographical Digression: Cornelius Connor (1799-1858)

MAUCH CHUNK INN.

THE Subscriber respectfully informs his friends and the public generally, that he has opened a new and commodious

PUBLIC HOUSE,

on the north side of Market Square, a few rods west of its junction with Berwick street, and in the immediate vicinity of the Lehigh Coal & Navigation Company's offices, and the several stores and principal Mechanics' shops in the place. Having prepared his House, stables, &c. with every thing necessary for the convenience and accommodation of Visiters, Travellers, and Teamsters, and furnished his bar with a good assortment of choice liquors, he will deem it a pleasure to wait upon all who may favor him with a call.

CORNELIUS CONNOR.

Mauch Chunk, June 15, 1833.-27.4f.

Mauch Chunk Courier,
10 Aug 1833, DML

CORNELIUS CONNOR arrived in Mauch Chunk in the early 1820s. In the early 1830s he partnered with various Mauch Chunk entrepreneurs to build canal boats. In 1833 he constructed the White Swan Inn, which was destroyed in Mauch Chunk's business district fire of July 1849. He rebuilt the hotel as The American House, which, although greatly modified, is still standing as the Inn at Jim Thorpe.

Although he operated his Mauch Chunk Hotel until his death in 1858, Conner's experience with contracting in the Panther Valley was short-lived, mining coal from Tunnel No. 8 for the season of 1846. Connor's daughter Elizabeth was married to Panther Valley mining contractor Thomas Broderick.[74]

Panther Valley Summary Timeline: 1846

➤ Spring 1846: Backtrack for returning empty coal cars to Summit Hill completed, using steam driven engines on Mt. Pisgah and Jefferson to haul trains of empty cars up the inclines using metal bands.

➤ Contractors complete construction of Panther Creek Inclined Plane No. 1, with link chains as hoisting mechanisms, and the railroad leading to this plane from Tunnel No. 1, passing Tunnels No. 3 and 4, although problems with the plane's machinery prevent it from hauling coal to the summit.

➤ Likely completion of "letting down" Plane No. 4, leading from the eastern end of the valley to the Summit of Sharp Mountain, just north of the Mt. Jefferson engine house.

➤ At a November 1846 meeting:
  o managers direct the driving of Slope No. 1 at the Summit.
  o managers request proposals for mining 60,000 tons of coal from Tunnel No. 1 and 30,000 tons from Slope No. 1

➤ At the November meeting the managers also awarded the following contracts for grading the remaining section of the Panther Valley railroad system:
  o Asa Lansford Foster, Robert Q. Butler and a Mr. Peter Dodson, to grade Section 1 of the railroad
  o Charles L. White and James Andrews, to grade Section 2 and 3

The Springvale Railroad

EXCEPT FOR A GRAVITY RETURN BACKTRACK, most of the Springvale Railroad was completed in 1846, including Panther Creek Plane No. 1, and a railroad leading from Tunnel No. 1 to the foot of this inclined plane, passing Tunnels No. 3 and 4. PC Plane No. 1, a steam-powered incline, went from a point part-way up the south side of the valley to the summit of Sharp Mountain.

Although grading and superstructure of PC Inclined Plane No. 1 were completed in 1846, actual use of the plane for hauling loaded cars was sporadic, due to severe problems with the hoisting mechanisms.

The Springvale backtrack was not constructed until 1848. From 1846 to 1848, the limited traffic over the road allowed the use of the temporary Springvale plane as a "letting down" plane, for returning empties to Tunnels 1, 3 and 4.

The Mystery of Panther Creek Plane No. 4

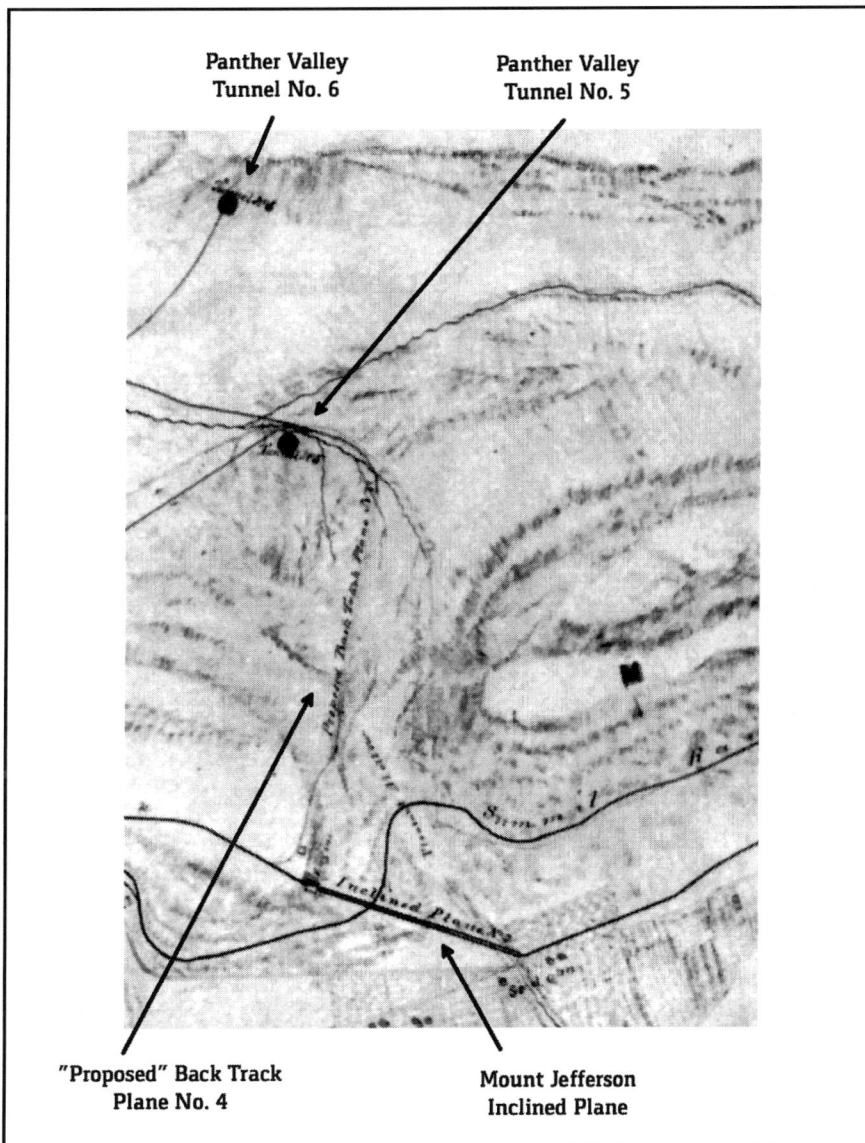

Panther Valley Tunnel No. 6

Panther Valley Tunnel No. 5

"Proposed" Back Track Plane No. 4

Mount Jefferson Inclined Plane

An enlarged section of the LC&N's Stockholder's 1845 map of the Panther Valley showing the "Proposed Back Track Plane No. 4." The graded bed of the inclined plane, and foundations for a small plane house are still visible on the mountain. Map adapted by author from John Hoffman 1845 LC&N Stockholder's Map

THE 1845 MAP of the Panther Valley shows a "Proposed Back Track Plane" on the east end of Panther Valley, leading from the Summit of Mount Jefferson to the valley floor near Tunnel No. 5.[75]

The existence of this inclined plane poses a mystery. Although there is no mention of its existence in any other LC&N records, another map, dating from the same period, surveyed by WF Roberts, also shows an inclined plane at that location.[76]

The 1845 Stockholder's map labels this plane a "Back Track" incline, indicating that it was a "letting down" plane, rather than a hoisting plane, most likely planned for lowering empties for Tunnels 5, 6 and 7 at the east end of the valley. It was also likely used for getting tools and supplies for the driving of these tunnels.

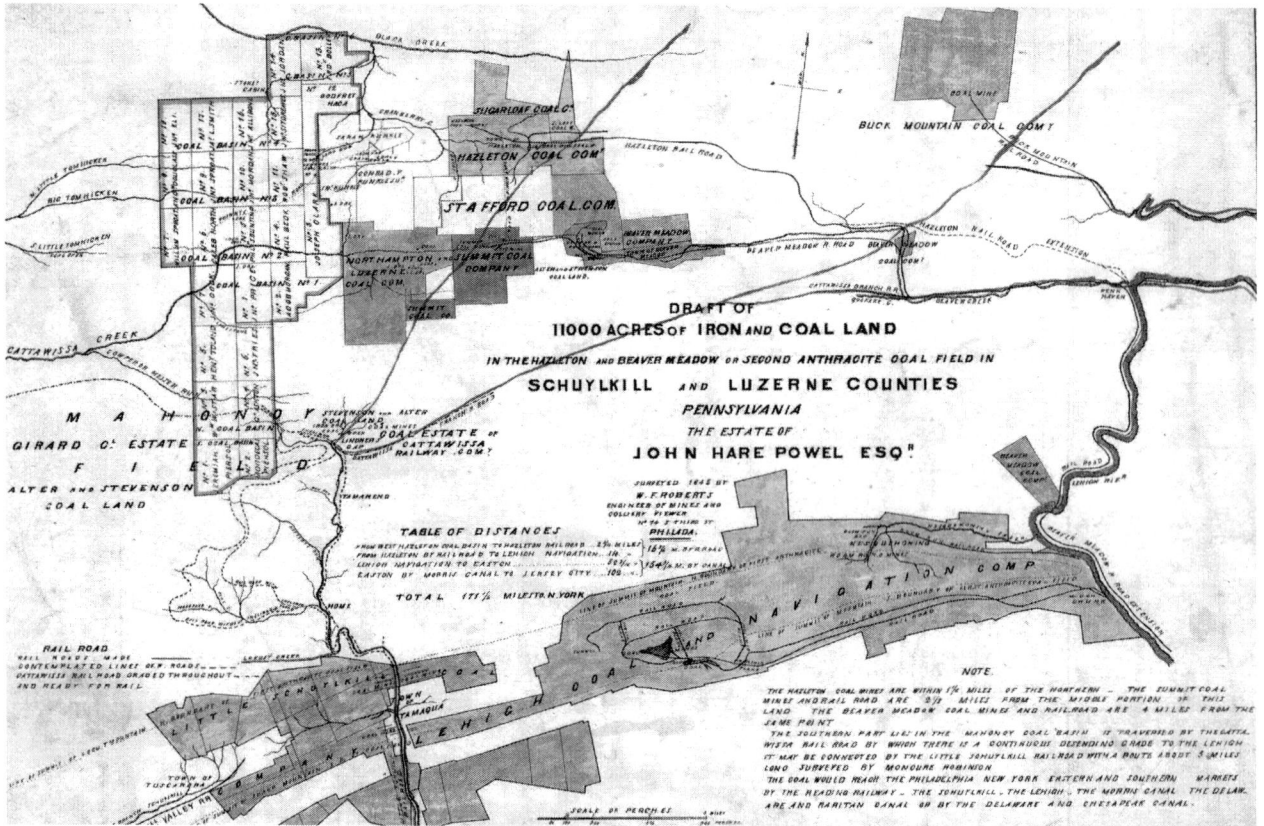

This map also shows Panther Valley Inclined Plane No. 4. "Draft of 11,000 Acres of Iron and Coal Land in the Hazelton and Beaver Meadow or Second Anthracite Coal Field in Schuylkill and Luzerne Counties Pennsylvania." The Estate of John Hare Powel, Esq. Surveyed 1845 by W. F. Roberts, Engineer of Mines and Colliery Viewer. Pennsylvania State Archives, RG-17, Map Book 1, Page 17

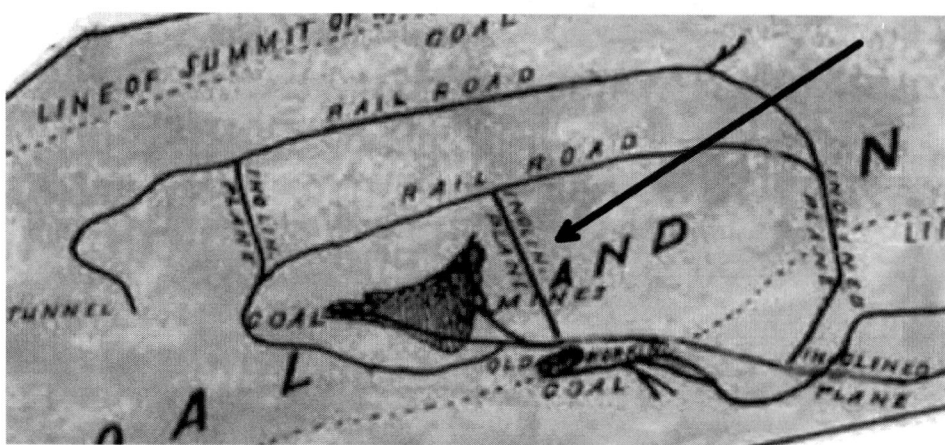

While the 1845 Stockholder's map shows this incline as a "proposed" plane, its actual existence is verifiable. The upper section of the single-track graded bed, as well as the foundation of the small plane house can still be found, north of the remains of the Mt. Jefferson engine house.

According to the late Jay Frantz, a long-time resident of Nesquehoning and LC&N employee, oral traditions had plane No. 4 hoisting coal to the summit of Mt. Jefferson sometime in 1845 and 1846.[77] However, there are several difficulties with these stories. First, the LC&N did not report the discovery of coal seams in the valley's eastern tunnels until early 1848, when Tunnel No. 5, which was driven into the mountainside near the foot of Plane No. 4, reached the Mammoth vein.[78]

More problematic is the lack of an ash pile. Although it is possible that coal mined from Tunnel No. 5 was hoisted to the summit over Plane No. 4 from April of 1848 until the completion of the Panther Creek Railroad in August of 1849, no ash bank can be found in the vicinity of the foundations of the No. 4 plane house, which does not appear to have been large enough to support a steam boiler and hoisting engine. An ash bank would provide evidence that a steam boiler had operated there.

One explanation for the lack of an ash bank at the head of Plane No. 4 is the later use of abandoned ash piles for road work following area snowstorms.

Sketch of the interior of a slope mine. *Harper's Weekly*, September 1857, "Coal and the Coal-Mines of Pennsylvania," 462

Slope No. 1

IN NOVEMBER 1846 the company directed the driving of a slope into the summit of the mountain southeast of the old quarry, but west of the newer Summit Quarry, into an opening made previously by George Kelso and Alexander McLean. Although located on the summit of Sharp Mountain, this was known as Panther Valley Slope No. 1. A steam engine used for a short time on the Mount Jefferson plane was transferred to the head of this slope.[79]

This was the first slope mine driven by the LC&N. Although the LC&N had approved a slope mine at Room Run as early as July of 1848, this was not driven until 1852.[80] A slope mine is driven down through a sloping vein, usually from the outcrop, so the driving of the slope itself produces marketable coal. Gangways are then driven horizontally, perpendicular to the slope.

An artist's conception of the entrance to Slope No. 1, driven near the Summit Mines in 1846. "Workings" off this slope were accidentally ignited in 1859 resulting in an underground fire that took over a century to extinguish. "The Coal-Beds of Pennsylvania," *Illustrated News*, 15 Jan 1854, 36

In the Annual Report for the year 1846, presented in May of 1847, the managers reported on the heavy expenditures required for the expansion into the Panther Creek Valley:

> The improvements begun within the last few years, and forming part of a connected, extended, and as it is believed, of a well devised system for the steady and progressive enlargement of the Company's business, are regularly carrying forward to completion; but it is not expected that the benefit, to arise from them, will begin to be fully realized prior to the year 1848. Some of the tunnels will, however, contribute materially to the present season's supply of coal.[81]

In spite of all the work done in 1846, according to the company's Annual Report for the year, no coal from any of the Panther Valley openings was sent to market.[82]

Biographical Digression: Charles Loomis White (1822 - 1880)

ACCORDING TO MATHEWS AND HUNGERFORD Charles L. White was the son of Canvass White, the renowned engineer of the Erie Canal and the man who engineered the lower section of the Lehigh Canal.[83] There is some dispute about this. In his treatment of Canvass White, the late Gerald Bastoni stated that Canvass White had only one son, named Hugh, who died in 1828.[84] Recently some additional facts have come to light, highly suggestive that the Charles L. White, who lived and worked in around Mauch Chunk and the Panther Valley, was indeed the son of the renowned Canvass White.

Mauch Chunk Census records provide some of these facts. These records show that Charles L. White had a son, born in 1863, whom he named Canvass. In addition, the 1860 census lists Charles

L. White living in Mauch Chunk and includes among his household a 55-year-old woman named Louisa. The renowned Canvass White was married to Louisa Loomis, a woman whom he left deeply in debt when he died in 1834. The final suggestive fact is that Charles White's middle name was Loomis.[85]

Research has shown that Canvass White left behind not only a son in Mauch Chunk, but also a daughter, Cornelia Porter White, who in 1852 married Rufus Henry Barnes, of Summit Hill.[86]

Besides taking contracts in the Panther Valley, between 1846 and 1849 Charles L. White partnered with Mauch Chunk's Nathan D. Cortright to drive and mine coal from the Hacklebernie Tunnel.[87]

In 1849 Charles L. White led a group of Mauch Chunk adventurers who sailed for California on the *Algoma*. White remained in the "gold regions" well into the 1850's, at one time operating a hotel, but in 1880 died in Mauch Chunk.[88] Another California migrant on that boat was Charles E. Foster, son of Asa Lansford Foster, and one of the publishers of the *Carbon County Gazette and Mauch Chunk Courier.*[89]

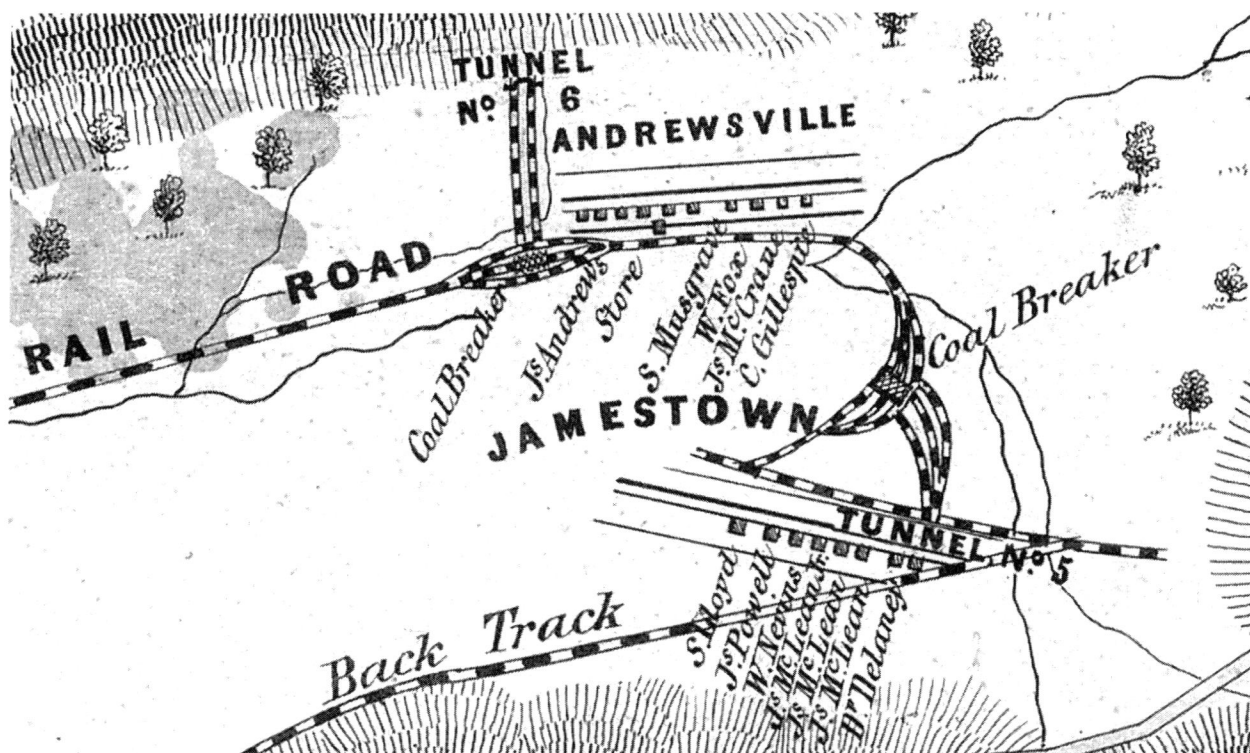

The Panther Valley patch towns of Andrewsville and Jamestown were established at the east end of the Panther Creek Valley in the early 1850s by James Andrews and James McLean respectively. Their homes are clearly shown on the map, adapted by the author from the 1854 Philip Nunan map. Also clearly shown are the Jamestown switch-backs that helped popularize the Panther Valley switch-back.

Biographical Digression: James Andrews (NA-NA)

WHILE MUCH IS KNOWN about men like John Leisenring, Charles L. White and others, little is known about James Andrews, other than the fact that he contracted in the Panther Valley and established the patch town of Andrewsville at the eastern end of the Valley. The name is a common one, so tracking this man throughout his life has been difficult.

After the construction of the Panther Creek Railroad, Andrews consistently received contracts to mine coal at Tunnel No. 6. He also received mining contracts at the Company's "Old Tunnel," later known as Hacklebernie. The patch town at the Tunnel No. 6 section was named "Andrewsville" after James Andrews. Although decades later incorporated into the Borough of Lansford, the small street and its homes are still known as Andrewsville to this day.[90]

Earlier, following the devastating January 1841 Flood, Andrews partnered with a man named Leslie to make repairs to the Upper Division of the Lehigh Canal.[91]

During construction of Asa Packer's LVRR, James Andrews, in partnership with Daniel Bertsch, Sr. received contractors for construction of Section 35 of the railroad.[92] In 1860, the LC&N awarded James Andrews the contract to grade and lay the superstructure of a railroad to and from the Dry Hollow slope. That railroad was never built.[93]

An early view of Andrewsville, a Panther Valley mining patch later consolidated into the borough of Lansford. The No. 6 breaker is visible in the distance. Courtesy of the National Canal Museum, a program of the Delaware & Lehigh National Heritage Corridor, Easton, PA

Panther Valley Summary Timeline: circa 1847

> 1846 & 1847: Unsuccessful testing of link chains on Panther Creek Plane No. 1.
> Early 1847: Slope No. 1 driven at the Summit.
> Spring 1847: "Turnout" of laborers on Panther Creek Railroad.
> Mining discontinued at Old Quarry due to exhaustion of the beds.
> Summer 1847: LC&N laid out patch town of Ashton.
> Fall of 1847: Wire ropes installed and tested on Inclined Plane No. 1.
> Engine foundation and housing for Panther Creek Plane No. 2 completed, and the engine itself placed under contract.
> Fall of 1847: LC&N managers ordered the construction of a water powered machine in Mauch Chunk for making wire ropes.
> October 1847: LC&N orders the construction of a railroad from Tunnel No. 2 to the foot of Panther Creek plane No. 2. This railroad was never built.

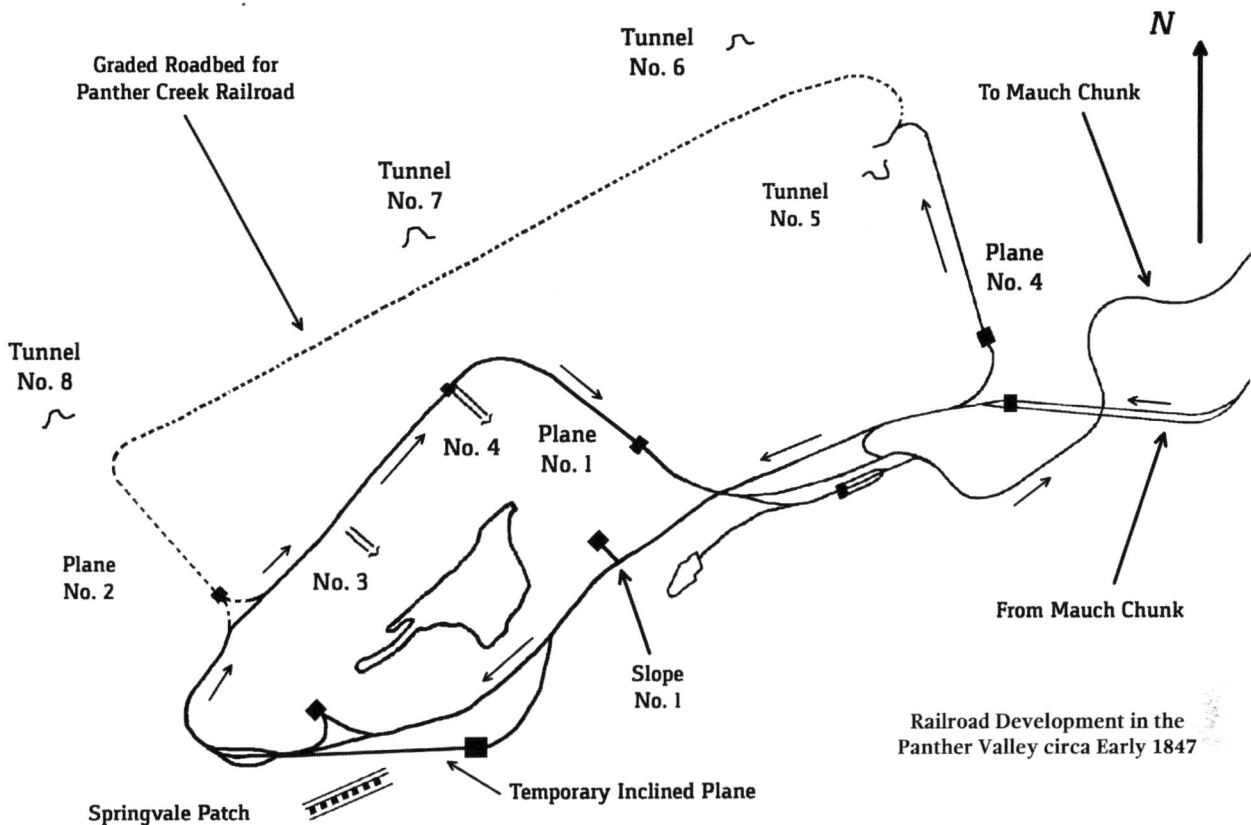

Railroad development at the Summit and in Panther Creek Valley circa 1847. Slope No. 1 was driven early in 1847. Loaded cars were hoisted to the Summit over Panther Creek Plane No. 1. After processing at the breaker, the coal traveled the original descending gravity railroad to the chutes on the Lehigh River. Plane No. 4 at the east end of the valley was a temporary inclined plane for lowering supplies to the east end of the valley for driving tunnels on the valley floor. Map adapted by the author from various sources

Difficulties with the Inclined Planes

THE LC&N BEGAN USING self-acting inclined planes in 1827, when the Mauch Chunk gravity railroad terminated at an inclined plane leading from a bluff overlooking Mauch Chunk to the Lehigh River. Several years later three self-acting inclined planes were installed on the Room Run Railroad. The simplistic designs for these planes and the light hoisting loads of empty cars allowed the use of hemp rope or link chains wound up around sprockets. As the LC&N system evolved to steam-powered inclined planes and heavier loads, problems began to emerge.

Panther Creek Plane No. 1 was approximately 2462 feet long with an elevation of 375 feet. The engine house for the plane was constructed 1730 feet from the foot of the plane and 732 feet from the head of the plane.[94] Plane No. 1 was designed with the engine house at the head of the plane. This design was quickly modified, moving the engine house part-way down the plane. Although the reasons for moving the engine house have not been recorded, it is easy to surmise that the change was made to allow gravity feed of the water supply from a spring on the summit of the mountain. Placing the engine house directly on the summit would have required pumping capabilities, complicating the engine design.

Although the LC&N began using iron bands for hoisting empty coal cars on the Pisgah and Jefferson planes as early as 1846, experimentation on the Ashley planes of the L&SRR showed that iron bands would not work for heavy loads.

39

The inclined planes generally worked well, but the straps have not fully realized our expectations; they proved to be too weak, and it has been found impracticable to get an equal tension on several straps laying side by side and connected together; so that, where there are several straps, as we have them, the weight most generally comes on one strap. The only remedy seems to be, either to get straps of sufficient strength, so that two connected together with a chain around a shieve (sic), shall convey the load, or to adopt wire ropes. As the latter are yet an experiment in this country, it will be advisable to wait until a fair trial shall be had with them, before incurring much expense to adopt them.[95]

Panther Creek Plane No. 1, therefore, was designed with a link chain wound around a steam-engine driven sprocket. This was not a new design, but one that had been used on the self-acting inclined planes of the Room Run Railroad until 1838, when they were replaced by iron bands. This was also the design undoubtedly used on the temporary Springvale inclined plane. [96]

A greatly simplified barney car waits at the foot of Panther Creek Plane No. 1 after it was double tracked. After link chains and sprockets were found to be unsatisfactory for hauling loaded coal cars to the Summit, Edwin Douglas conducted experiments with wire ropes on the inclined plane. The bridge crossing the plane a short distance in front of the barney carried loaded cars from Slope No. 4, driven in 1859. This track was added in Spring of 1861. Courtesy Bob Gormley

The barney cars on the Panther Creek inclined planes did not have collapsible axles as did those on Mount Pisgah and Mount Jefferson. Instead, loaded coal cars were shunted in front of the safety car on graded "lead in" tracks. In this view from a Kleckner stereopticon, a loaded coal car waits to be shunted in front of the barney from the left "lead-in" track at the foot of Panther Creek Plane No. 2. The culm banks visible at the top left are probably the spoil banks from Slope No. 2. Development of the lead-in track concept courtesy of Harry Murphy. Photo courtesy of Bob Gormley

However, chains frequently broke at their weakest link. This had been a problem even on the Room Run railroad, where in 1834 one of the links on the river plane broke. Link chains had to be wound up around sprockets, and the sprockets themselves did the most damage.[97]

During testing of Panther Creek Plane No. 1 in late 1846 and early 1847 the link chain proved so troublesome that wire ropes for both Panther Creek planes No. 1 and 2 were ordered from the works of John Roebling. These ropes did not arrive until the middle of 1847.

Owing to the delays in transporting the wire rope on the State works, it did not arrive until July. . . There are some slight alterations yet to be made to suit the working of the rope, which will be done, ready for use in the spring.[98]

41

A newspaper reporter observed one of these ropes passing through Mauch Chunk on its way to the Panther Creek Valley:

> A wire rope intended for a plane at Summit Hill, passed through our town a few days since drawn by ten mules. So great was its weight probably seven or eight tons that several chains were broken in front of our office, although the ground is nearly level.[99]

In August of 1847 the wire rope finally arrived and was installed on Inclined Plane No. 1. Full operation of the plane occurred three months later, following testing of the wire rope.[100]

Despite laudatory remarks by the LC&N Managers within their Annual Report, there were complications with the wire ropes. Robert Sayre, as the company engineer on site, had to contend with these problems. Sayre began keeping a succinct diary on January 4, 1851, while he was on location in the Valley. His notes included brief descriptions of problems encountered with the Valley's mining mechanisms.

Between January 4, 1851 and May 5, 1852, his last day of work in the Panther Valley, Sayre recorded six breakages of the main ropes on the Panther Creek inclined Planes, three on Plane No. 1 and three on Plane No. 2. Sayre recorded other problems with the ropes, as well, including the separation of rope strands and the rope coming off its sheave wheel. Sometimes a rope could be "mended." Other failures required the complete replacement of the rope, shutting down the railroad for days at a time.

Sayre's last day working for the LC&N was May 5, 1852. That day the rope broke yet again on Panther Creek Plane No. 2. Sayre spent the next day packing up his belongings to move to Mauch Chunk, ready to begin work surveying the dream railroad of Asa Packer.[101]

By the beginning of the 1870s it was still necessary to replace the wire ropes every year.

Labor Troubles Begin

IN 1847 A SUBSTANTIAL AMOUNT of work was completed on the Panther Valley railroad system, despite a "turnout" of the railroad laborers on March 1st of that year, possibly the earliest recorded strike in the Panther Creek region. According to the editor of the *Carbon County Gazette*,

> . . . they will be sent to seek employment where they can be better satisfied. The wages which they were receiving were higher than those paid to the miners upon the summit, and the contractors have been obliged to send hundreds of men from their doors, who came seeking employment, when they had no room to accommodate them. Laborers have never been more plenty than they are at present, and from the reports of the number of immigrants monthly arriving, there is every reason to believe that they will continue to flock to all the public works where their services may be required. The wages therefore will be lower than they were last season.[102]

Labor disputes within the valley would grow over the years, intensifying in the years leading up to and following the Civil War. These problems would continue until mining was discontinued in the valley in the twentieth century.

Completion of the Panther Creek Railroad System

VALLEY CONTRACTS SIGNED in December 1846 resulted in completion of the remaining section of the Panther Valley railroad system designed to service Tunnels 5 through 8. Asa Lansford Foster, Robert Q. Butler, Peter Dodson, Charles L. White and James Andrews received contracts for grading the railroad.[103]

This work included grading and laying the superstructure of Inclined Plane No. 2, later known as the Coaldale plane. Panther Creek Plane No. 2 was smaller than plane No. 1, with a length of approximately 2030 feet and an elevation of 250 feet. In 1847 the engine foundation and housing were completed, and the engine itself placed under contract, to be delivered in the spring of 1848. The engine house rested at the head of the plane; the water source for the steam engine being a spring located near Tunnel No. 1.[104]

Looking down into the Panther Valley as a barney car nears the head of Panther Creek Plane No. 2. The safety devices of the Panther Valley barney cars were patterned after those on the Mount Jefferson inclined plane. They did not use the center rail, "cat-step" and safety latch found on the Mount Pisgah inclined plane, but instead used the dubious "outrigger legs." Bob Gormley

Panther Creek Plane No. 2, which hoisted loaded coal cars from the valley floor to a location midway up the mountainside, intersected the Springvale railroad between Tunnel No. 1 and Tunnel No. 3. Besides hoisting loaded cars to the summit, for a time the plane was also used for letting down empties for Tunnel No. 8.

In late 1847 the LC&N awarded contracts for the 1848 season for mining at Tunnels No. 1, 3 and 4, as well as slope No. 1.[105] Tunnels No. 2, 5, 6, 7 and 8 continued to be driven during 1847, such that by January 1, 1848 the tunnels had been driven the following lengths:

Table 1 Panther Valley Tunnel Lengths Driven by 1848 (from LC&N Annual Report for 1847, 24)	
Tunnel No. 1	Mammoth struck previously
Tunnel No. 2	340 yards
Tunnel No. 3	Mammoth struck previously
Tunnel No. 4	Mammoth struck previously
Tunnel No. 5	276 yards (mammoth reached 1848)
Tunnel No. 6	278 yards
Tunnel No. 7	315 yards
Tunnel No. 8	321 yards

In all, in 1847 the company expended $69,343.73 on construction work in the Panther Valley, including a new engine and wire rope for plane No. 1. Edwin Douglas anticipated full operation of the completed railroad by July 1848.[106]

Panther Valley Summary Timeline: 1848

➢ Spring of 1848: The LC&N began allowing passengers to travel into the valley.

➢ Early 1848: The "temporary" inclined plane at Springvale dismantled.

➢ Early 1848: The "First Return Backtrack" passing Tunnel No. 1 and utilizing the soon to be famous "Switch-Backs," was completed.

➢ To accommodate the replacement of the link chain with wire rope, the steam driven sprocket on Plane No. 1 was replaced with a grooved "sheave."

➢ July 1848: LC&N's wire rope factory put in operation on Susquehanna Street in Mauch Chunk.

➢ During 1848 the LC&N moved screening and sorting coal from the river schutes to the coal breakers at the mines.

Passenger Service on the New Railroad

IN SPRING 1848, while the Panther Valley railroad system was nearing completion and the famous valley "switch-backs" had yet to be constructed, the LC&N began allowing passenger cars, to descend into the valley. (See Appendix A).[107]

The "Switch-Back" - Panther Valley's First Return Backtrack

THAT SAME YEAR, as Panther Creek Plane No. 1 came fully online and production increased at Tunnels 1, 3 and 4, the temporary inclined plane at Springvale proved unsatisfactory for the letting down of empties. That year the plane was replaced by a backtrack into the valley, part of the original design. Douglas reported that the road "has fully answered the purpose for which it was intended."[108]

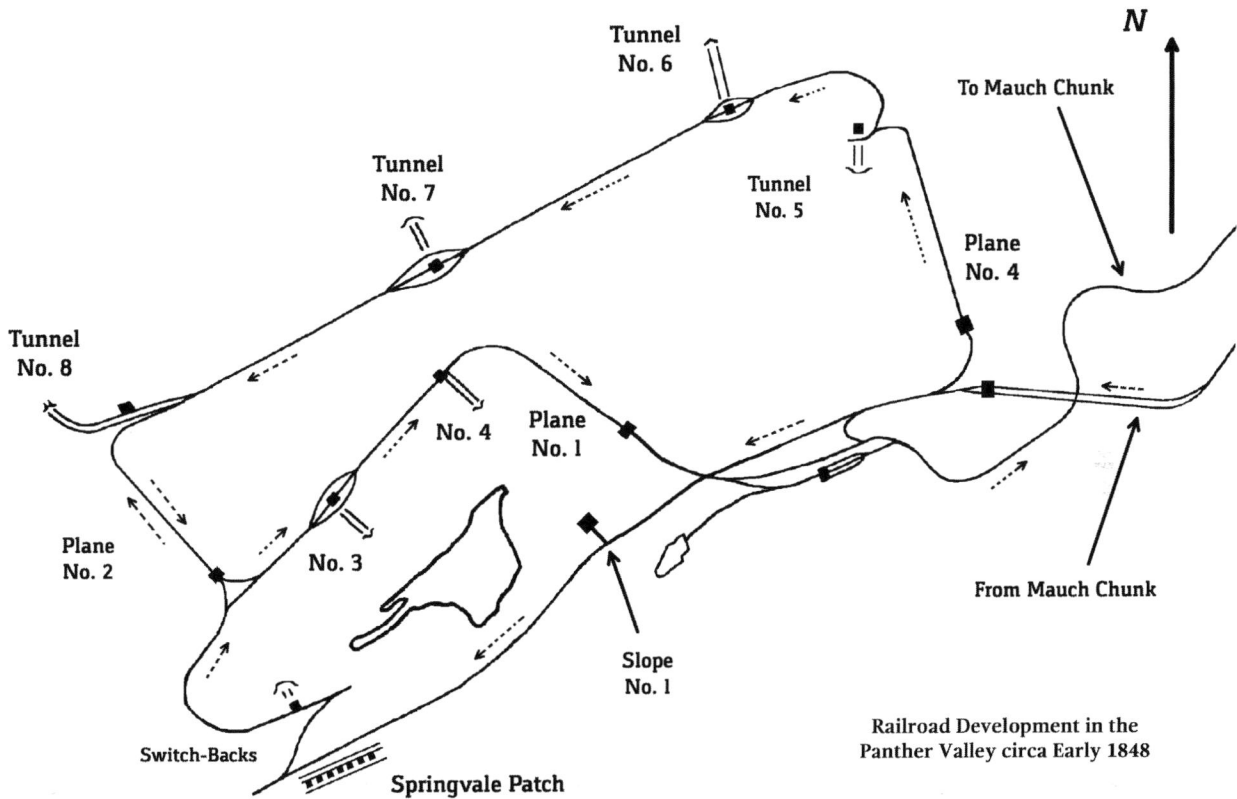

Railroad Development in the
Panther Valley circa Early 1848

Panther Valley Railroad development circa 1848. In 1848 the temporary Springvale inclined plane was replaced by a backtrack into the valley, utilizing the "kickback" switches that gave the railroad its nickname, "The Switch-Back." Plane No. 4 was likely still in operation to "let down empties for valley tunnels 5 through 8, although empties were also let down Plane No. 2.

The Springvale "return backtrack" descended west into the valley from the Summit, past the newer "Summit Mines" and the old Quarry. It utilized two of the self-acting "kickback switches" that gave the railroads in the Panther Creek Valley the unique designation "Switch-Back." (See Appendices B & C). As noted by Switchback afficionado Walt Niehoff:

> Now, we unfortunately don't know what mechanism they used to achieve the self-acting-ness. Certainly, all they needed was some "springiness" to hold the turnout in the downhill-going branch. Wheel pressure would have aligned the switch points when the car entered the turnout in the converging direction and the springiness would have aligned it downhill when the car entered in the diverging direction. What could they have used to get the springiness? Probably not a helical spring; a bending member would have been simpler.[109]

According to local tradition, these automatic switches were employed so that empty cars could drift down the mountainside without the need for brakemen. However, they did not work in this manner, but instead permitted a shallower grade on a steep mountainside. The steepness of the grade still required mechanical brakes and the men to operate them.

Indeed, reports of accidents on the Panther Valley "Back-Tracks" indicate the absolute need for the brakes, and the dangers when the brakes failed.

> We learn that a serious accident happened at Summit Hill last Tuesday morning, resulting in one death and the injury of over twenty others. A number of workmen proceeded on trucks down the switch-back, in the morning to go to work, and owing to the frost on the rails and car wheels, the brakes did not work, and the whole party went down the grade at a fearful rate, which resulted in the accident.[110]

This Panther Valley section of the 1854 Philip Nunan Map shows the Springvale switch-backs in clear detail. LC&N Assistant Engineer George Washington Salkeld designed these automatically acting switches that allowed a reasonable descent down the steep mountainside. The switches were used for only a short period of time and were then replaced by a descending grade that more closely followed the contour of the mountainside. Adapted by author from the 1854 Philip Nunan Map.

The abandonment of the original temporary inclined plane at Springvale increased traffic over Panther Creek plane No. 1, as it would now be handling loaded cars from Tunnel No. 1, as well as previously from Tunnels No. 3 and 4. This required an increase of power as well as other "adjustments." In 1848, to accommodate the replacement of the link chain with wire rope, the steam driven sprocket on Plane No. 1 was replaced with a grooved "sheave". The sheave was a metal wheel with grooved rims for guiding the wire rope to lay evenly as it was wound up. This method tended to damage the rope, and as a result, in 1849 the sheave or friction wheels were replaced with wooden drums.[111]

The Success of the Wire Rope

PANTHER VALLEY INCLINED PLANES No. 1 and No. 2 used a hoisting scheme similar to that used on the Mount Pisgah and Mount Jefferson inclines of the original gravity railroad. That is, instead of hauling loaded cars up the inclines by cables attached to the front of the loaded car, the loads were "pushed" up the inclines by "barney" cars themselves attached to the hoisting engines by wire ropes. This saved labor by not requiring laborers to attach and detach cables for each of the loaded cars.

The use of wire rope on Panther Creek Plane No. 1 proved to be the most successful of all the hoisting mechanisms tested by the LC&N. As a result, in the Fall of 1847 LC&N managers ordered the construction of a water powered machine for making wire ropes.[112]

This building, the precursor to the present-day Hooven building on Susquehanna Street in Jim Thorpe, was originally a grist mill, constructed by the LC&N. In 1848 it was converted into a factory for making wire ropes. The wire rope factory was later removed to West Broadway and eventually relocated to Wilkesbarre.

In July of 1848 this machine was put in operation on Susquehanna Street in Mauch Chunk, the work of Edwin Douglas, George Washington Salkeld and Robert H. Sayre. According to Donald Sayenga, this was America's first indoor wire rope factory. The machine was started at midnight on July 3, 1848.[113]

> The spools of strands, seven in number, had previously been prepared, and were placed in the machine, and by seven o'clock the following morning, a rope one thousand seven hundred and thirty-four feet in length was twisted and ready for the plane, upon which it was placed and in operation on the 4th. The rope is one and a half inches in diameter and is composed of 133 lengths of wires.[114]

47

The rope was a test rope for Panther Creek Plane No. 1. Since it was only 1734 feet long, it would only reach from the bottom of the inclined plane to the engine house, located part way up the plane. But the experiment proved a success, and the company began manufacturing ropes for both planes within the Panther Valley.

The wire-rope on Plane No. 1 continues to work satisfactorily, and, from its present appearances, I conclude it will last one, if not two more seasons.[115]

Mauch Chunk photographer James Zellner shot this picture of the interior of a wire rope factory, possibly the Mauch Chunk establishment after it was relocated to West Broadway

The use of wire ropes on the Panther Creek planes continued until the planes were abandoned. In 1858, when Henry Darwin Rogers completed Pennsylvania's First Geological Survey, he reported that the Panther Creek planes utilized wire ropes 1 3/8 inches in diameter, containing 36 strands of No. 14 wire, and that one foot of cable weighed 1 pound. The wire ropes were strong enough to haul loaded coal cars up the Panther Creek inclines in sets of three.[116]

In his diary entry for December 31, 1851, Robert Sayre noted that Panther Creek Plane No. 1 required 2 ropes: a "back rope" measuring 2740 feet and a "long rope" 3468 feet long. These observations are hard to understand since, unlike the inclined planes on Mt. Pisgah and Mt. Jefferson, there is little information on their construction.

For instance, we know that tension on the Pisgah and Jefferson safety cars was maintained by connecting the back ends of the safety cars to a counterweight ballast car. However, while photographs of the Panther Valley inclined plane safety cars reveal a wire rope at the rear of the car, there is no information as to the mechanism for counterweighting.

It is easy to conclude that the "long rope" was used for pulling the safety car up the plane and wound up around a wooden drum as the safety car ascended the plane. This wire rope most likely passed from the hoisting drum, beneath the incline, upward to the head of the plane. There it passed over a pulley and descended the plane to the front of the safety car. Since the engine house was located 732 feet from the head of the plane, and the plane itself was 2462 feet long, the "long rope" had to be at least 3194 feet long (2462 ft. + 732 feet). The remaining 274 feet of rope could have been merely slack.

The "back rope," being 2740 feet (278 feet longer than the plane) was most likely attached from the rear of the car to a counterweight, of some fashion. The ballast car, used on the Pisgah and Jefferson inclines, was probably not used on the Panther Creek planes until they were double-tracked (1856-1857).[117]

The LC&N also began using wire ropes on the schutes at Mauch Chunk as early as the winter of 1848-49, when the hemp ropes on all the chutes were replaced with the new ropes.[118] Wire ropes were also used on the inclined planes of the slope mines.

The wire ropes were heavy, and, of course, challenging to transport. Before locomotive railroads connected the Panther Creek Valley with the remainder of the world, these ropes, which broke all too frequently, had to be transported from the factory at Mauch Chunk to the Panther Valley by horse or mule drawn wagon.

The following newspaper account reveals the difficulty:

A Heavy Drag. On Wednesday last we saw the largest team we ever beheld, employed in drawing a coil of wire rope from the wire factory in this borough for the use of one of the collieries in the neighborhood. The rope was wound upon a wooden drum, and weighed we were informed eleven tons. The team consisted of nineteen mules and two horses, and was employed from about seven o'clock until eleven in dragging it from the wire factory to the market house, a distance of less than half a mile.[119]

The wire ropes also presented tripping hazards to the civilians who dared to cross over the inclined planes.

Fatal Accident. Mrs. Mullin, wife of Wm. Mullin, of the village of Ashton, when crossing panther Creek Plane No. 1 this afternoon, with water, fell upon the track, and the safety car ran over her and mangled her dreadfully, so that she died shortly after. It is supposed that she tripped when stepping over the back rope and so stunned by the fall that she was unable to get up or off the track before the car reached her.[120]

This coal breaker for Tunnel No. 5 was constructed in 1868 and torn down in 1902. The breaker sat on the Panther Creek Railroad between Tunnel No. 5 and Tunnel No. 6. A mine locomotive was introduced into Tunnel No. 5 the same year this breaker was completed. Bob Gormley

The Market Rules

ALTHOUGH EDWIN DOUGLASs and the LC&N managers had predicted large production from the Panther Creek mines in 1848, things did not go as planned, as the market was unable to handle the company's desired level of production. In July of that year, the Board ordered curtailment of all operations.

According to Douglas:

> Early in the season we received instructions from the Managers to suspend all operations and expenditures, not strictly necessary for the prosecution of our regular business, and the preservation of the works. Could we have continued and completed the unfinished work . . . we should have been prepared to send forward, next season, not less than 400,000 tons of coal.[121]

A group of miners pose in front of an early tunnel in the Panther Creek Valley, in a photo from a Joseph Brown stereoview

In the same annual report, the Managers blamed the shutdown of the works as necessary, due to the

> ill-judged system of a sliding-scale of charges adopted, and the pernicious credits allowed, during the past year, by the rival companies on the Schuylkill. The natural and necessary consequences of these measures, and of the unnatural stimulus thus given to production, soon exhibited themselves in a market gorged to repletion, and in the rapid and early accumulation of stocks in the face of a languid demand from consumers.[122]

The effects, as noted in the same report, were reduced prices. Presumably the LC&N's biggest gripe was that the increased production of coal came from the Schuylkill region and not the Lehigh. The lower prices also thwarted the company's plans to use increased sales of coal to meet debt service.

Despite the Managers request, Douglas anticipated a better market in the years to come, and vigorously pushed the development of the additional mines. The LC&N spent a total of $24,446.61 on these tunnels during 1848, however, only Tunnels No. 2 and 6 were to reach the Mammoth vein that year.[123] In spite of the Panther Valley railroad system being completed enough to allow coal to move to market, additional modifications were planned.

Table 2 Panther Valley Tunnel Lengths Driven in 1848 (from LC&N Annual Report for 1848, 21)	
Tunnel No. 2	423 yards
Tunnel No. 5	282 yards
Tunnel No. 6	347 yards
Tunnel No. 7	449 yards
Tunnel No. 8	478 yards

As the tunnels stretched towards the Mammoth vein, Douglas reported that before they could produce marketable coal, "breaking and screening machinery" would have to be erected, as well as necessary railroad sidings. He estimated the cost at about $10,000 per tunnel. Production from the company's Panther Creek operations increased to an output of 214,839 tons of coal in 1848, from approximately 202,000 tons in 1847. Douglas revised his prediction of full operation of the Panther Creek Railroad to March of 1849.[124]

Breaking and Screening the Coal

IN 1848 THE LC&N'S METHODS of processing coal underwent a major change.

> In consequence of complaints of the bad condition of our prepared coal, as sent to market, it was deemed advisable to change the system; and to break, screen and assort the coal at the mines, instead of breaking it at the mines, and screening and assorting it at the landing, as heretofore practiced.[125]

As a result, "breaking and screening fixtures" later simply known as "breakers" were constructed for the Summit Mines, Slope No. 1, as well as Tunnels No. 1, 3 and 4 at a cost of $33,400.35.[126] This equipment was placed in service by May of 1848 and Douglas hoped that

> the coal will now go to market in such a condition, that it will puzzle the most fastidious to find grounds of complaint.[127]

Biographical Digression: James McLean (1824-1864)

JAMES MCLEAN was the first son of Alexander McLean. He followed his father into the coal mining business in and around Summit Hill, taking over mining contracts at the Springvale Tunnel No. 1 after his father retired.[128] In January of 1850 McLean took a three year mining contract for Tunnel No. 5, his next mining contract.[129] He settled in the No. 5 area of the Valley, and established the patch of "Jamestown," where he lived until his untimely death. In December of 1855 McLean was also awarded the contract to mine coal from Tunnels No. 7 & 8, in partnership with Jonathan

Simpson.[130] McLean also assisted in the reconstruction of the Lehigh Navigation following the June 1862 flood.[131]

In late 1863 James McLean was involved in a terrible accident on the Summit Hill and Mauch Chunk gravity railroad.

> On Monday morning last, as Mr. James McLean, with another gentleman, was coming down from Summit Hill on a truck, and as they neared the "five-mile tree," the truck jumped off the track, and was turned over, and the occupants thrown out very violently. Mr. McLean was very severely injured, one of his arms broken in two places, his head very badly bruised, and his tongue nearly cut off.[132]

McLean's arm soon required amputation, and he died a few months later.[133]

Slatepickers pose at the foot of schute No. 1 at Mauch Chunk. Although the LC&N used breakers and slatepickers at the mines, waste material still made its way down the gravity railroad. To alleviate consumer complaints, the LC&N employed old men and young boys on the chutes to manually remove any slate before the coal was loaded into canal boats. The wooden trough leading from the middle of the photo to the lower left carried water from the upper dam to the lower dam. Water flowing through the trough removed coal dirt from the chutes and deposited it below the lower dam, allowing the "dirt tracks" to be eliminated. Ray Holland

Panther Valley Summary Timeline: 1849

- ➤ 1849 was the first year that Panther Valley coal made it to market.
- ➤ Spring 1849: Tunnel No. 8 reached the Mammoth Vein.
- ➤ July 1849: Construction contract awarded to Myron N. Ingersoll, for building a second return backtrack from the summit to the valley floor.
- ➤ August 1849: Panther Creek Inclined Plane No. 2 completed.
- ➤ During 1849: Coal breakers completed at Tunnels 5 and 6.
- ➤ Fall 1849: LC&N began leasing lots in the mining patch of Ashton.
- ➤ Fall 1849. LC&N began extending mining contracts for 3 years vs 1 year.

Expansion of Mining in the Valley

IN EARLY SPRING OF 1849 Tunnel No. 8 reached the Mammoth vein.[134] By August additional sections of the Panther Creek Railroad, including Plane No. 2 were completed, and used until the season close.[135] However, satisfactory arrangements for returning empties to Tunnels 5, 6 and 7 on the valley floor, were not ready at that time. Several years later Henry Darwin Rogers, the State Geologist visited the scene and reported that empties for Tunnel No. 8 were "let down" Panther Creek Plane No. 2.[136]

It is possible that empties for the remaining tunnels were also let down Plane No. 2 and then hauled by mules up the slight grade to these tunnels. But this could only be a temporary solution since the railroad was single tracked and this would have resulted in traffic jams. It is also possible that Plane No. 4 was still in existence and used as a "letting down" plane. Another possibility is that a section of track, shown on the 1845 Stockholder's map, connected the foot of Plane No. 1 with the Tunnel No. 5 area, allowing the empties for Tunnels 5 through 7 to use the Springvale backtrack.

During 1849 coal breakers were completed at Tunnels 6 and 8. The breakers for Tunnels 5 and 7 were completed in early Spring of 1850.[137]

In 1849 LC&N coal production increased to 276,501 tons as additional valley mines came online. This was most likely the first year that coal from the Panther Valley went to market. The Company's Annual Report for the year, published on May 7, 1850 made the first reference to coal from the ". . . Tunnels recently brought into operation." [138]

The completion of the Panther Creek Railroad, as well as all the valley tunnels in 1849, permitted the LC&N to contract for longer periods of time. As a result, the Company signed 3-year mining contracts, for the years 1850, 1851 and 1852.[139]

Table 3 Panther Valley Mining Contracts for 1850 thru 1852 inclusive	
Contractor(s)	Mines
Daniel Bertsch	Tunnels No. 3, 4 and 7
James McLean	Tunnel No. 5
James Andrews	Tunnel No. 6
Thompson Peckens & James Steel	Tunnel No. 8

Mules pull loaded coal wagons out of Panther Valley coal mine Tunnel No. 8. Tourist trips around the valley sometimes included a tour of this mine, which was driven by Cornelius Conner. Conner also constructed Mauch Chunk's White Swan Inn, later known as the American Hotel and most recently, the Inn at Jim Thorpe. In the twentieth century Tunnel No. 8 became the Lehigh Coal and Navigation Company's showpiece

The Patch Towns of the Panther Valley

Office of The Lehigh Coal & Nav. Co.
Mauch Chunk, November 23, 1849.
PROPOSALS will be recieved at this Office until Saturday the 8th Dec., for furnishing all the materials and constructing 40 blocks of Dwelling Houses, at the Coal Mines in Panther Creek Valley. Plans and specifications can be seen at this Office.

E. A. DOUGDAS,
Sup't. and Engineer.

3—2

From the *Carbon Democrat*, 1 Dec 1849, DML

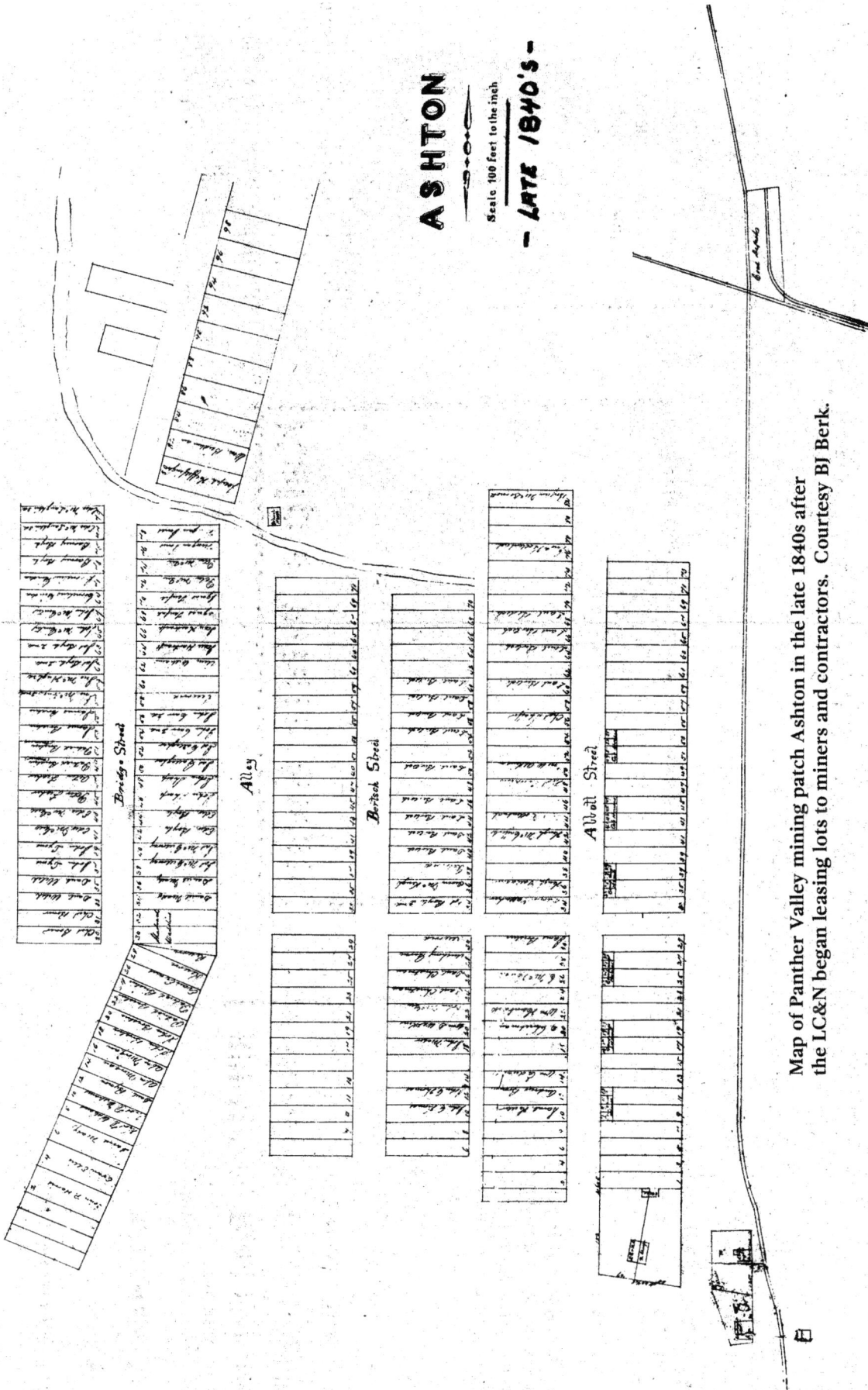

Map of Panther Valley mining patch Ashton in the late 1840s after the LC&N began leasing lots to miners and contractors. Courtesy BJ Berk.

WHILE SETTLERS HAD BEEN sporadically moving to the Panther Creek Valley for several decades, it wasn't until the late 1840's that the LC&N began officially leasing lots. And while the LC&N had been selling lots in Easton, Mauch Chunk and Nesquehoning since the early 1830s, the LC&N would not begin the sale of lots in the Panther Valley for many years to come. This may have been due to the mineral wealth underlying the LC&N property in the Panther Valley.

The first lease recorded in the Panther Valley was in the first official "Patch Town" of Ashton, located just to the northwest of the foot of Panther Creek inclined plane No. 1. The lease, approved by the LC&N Board of Managers on September 7, 1849 went to

Daniel Bertsch: for Lot No. 64 & 66, Abbott Street, in the Village of Ashton, term 15 years, rent $2 per annum. [140]

The Ashton patch had been laid out two years earlier, in the summer of 1847. Soon most of the valley contractors would begin leasing plots of ground and building houses on the lots.[141]

[Above] LC&N company-built homes on the north side of the 600 block on East Ridge Street in this 1902 photo. Smokestacks at the No. 6 Colliery are visible in the background to the left. As indicated on the map of Ashton on the preceding page, Ridge Street was originally Bridge Street.

[Top of Next Page] A company-built house as it appeared in 1902, when the Company did an audit of all property. The LC&N paid for the construction of Company homes, and then charged a monthly rent based upon the cost of construction at a rate of return of 6%. For example, if the house cost $600 to build, an annual rate of return of $36 was charged, or $3 per month. Note the towering culm banks behind the home

Panther Valley Summary Timeline: 1850

➤ Spring 1850: Breakers completed at Tunnels 5 and 7.

➤ Spring 1850: Panther Valley second return backtrack to eastern end of the Valley at Tunnel No. 5 completed.

➤ Slope No. 2 driven at the summit on the northwest slope of the Old Quarry.

➤ Construction of railroad yard and car stands at Summit Hill, east of the Old Quarry and Summit Mines.

➤ In 1850 Valley coal production reached all-time high of 330,447 tons.

Another "Switch-back" - Panther Valley's Second Return Backtrack

ALTHOUGH IT HAD NOT BEEN PART of the original design for the Panther Valley, in June of 1849 Edwin Douglas proposed a second backtrack to the valley floor estimating its cost at $4,929.41 subject to a reduction of $2500 for the use of old rail and materials on hand. It is highly likely that these old materials came from the abandonment and dismantlement of the temporary Springvale inclined plane, as well as from letting down plane No. 4.[142]

The contract for grading this backtrack, which led directly from the summit to the eastern end of the Panther Valley at Tunnel No. 5, was awarded to Myron N. Ingersoll on July 7, 1849, and was completed and in operation by April of 1850.[143] This backtrack also used self-acting switches, and so became part of the famous "Switch-back" railroad, being called the "New Switch-back." The original backtrack, leading past Springvale, was referred to as the "Old Switch-back." [144]

The use of the new section of track eliminated the need to lower empty cars down Plane No. 2, and may have contributed to the company's coal production, which increased to an all-time high of 330,447 tons for the year 1850.

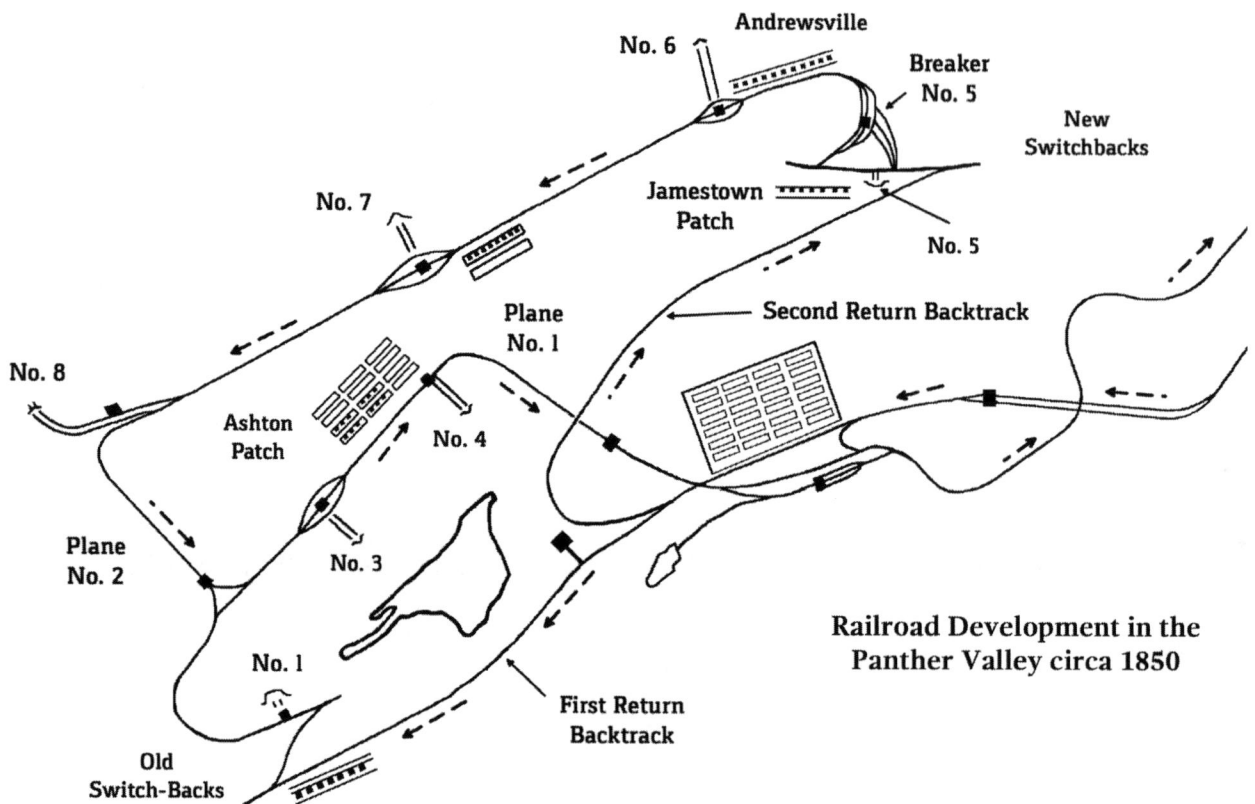

Railroad Development in the Panther Valley circa early 1850. Note that Inclined Plane No. 4 has been removed. Empties descended to the eastern end of the valley on a new return backtrack leading from the summit to Tunnel No. 5, where two new Switch-Backs were located. Map adapted by the author from the 1854 Philip Nunan Map, and other sources.

Biographical Digression: Myron N. Ingersoll (1804-1860)

MYRON INGERSOLL, although he constructed an important part of the Panther Valley system, was yet another Panther Valley contractor of limited information, and died, in 1860, as the result of an accident on the section of the Switch-Back that he built.

> Fatal Accident. On Monday afternoon last an accident happened on the switch-back railroad, which resulted in the death of Mr. Myron Ingersoll, of Summit Hill. He was running four cars loaded with sills, and when near the switch a set of cars came on behind, at full speed, and violently struck the sills, pitching Mr. Ingersoll some fifteen feet into the air, breaking his leg, fracturing his skull and otherwise injuring him so as to cause death in one hour. The deceased was an intelligent and worthy man, and leaves a wife and six children.[145]

The Switch-Back Railroad

ONE OF THE MOST INTERESTING FEATURES of the Panther Creek railroad and its return backtracks was the use of the "Y" or "kickback" switches, especially that the use and operation of them should become so well known. The switches were marvels to the tourists who traveled over the railroad to visit the mines in the Panther Creek Valley.

According to Christopher Northington at the Genealogy Desk of the Dimmick Memorial Library, the Panther Valley gravity railroad system instigated the use of the English word "Switch-Back" as a railroad term. (See Appendix B)

As the name of "Switch-Back" caught on, the whole of the LC&N's gravity railroad from Summit Hill to Mauch Chunk, and branches, came to be known by this name. Even though the Summit Hill and Mauch Chunk Gravity Railroad no longer descended into the Panther Creek Valley after 1872, the railroad continued to be known as the Switch-Back (also sp Switchback) a name by which it is known to this day.

This sketch is the only image of the Panther Valley switchbacks known to exist (other than images on maps). The view is from the breaker No. 5 area. Tunnel No. 5 is visible in the left-center of the view. Empty cars descended from the summit from the top-center of the sketch toward the center left, above the tunnel, where they "switched-back" and descended to the right-center of the view. M.S. Henry, *History of the Lehigh Valley*, 360

If not for the book, The *History of the Lehigh Valley* by M.S. Henry, we would know little about these switches.

> At Summit Hill . . . "The celebrated Switch-Back Railroad commences here, and runs through Panther Creek Valley to the different mines . . . We will now take our seats in an open car, from which we can better enjoy the view. Another push, and away we go down the first section of the switch-back, descending at the rate of 221 feet to the mile. But we now have a novel variation in the descent, instead of running in one direction down the side of the mountain to the bottom of the valley, the car zigzags back and forth, now we are riding with one end of the car in front, and then, as we change to another track, the other end of the car is in front.
>
> The change from one track to the other is made by a curious and ingenious self-acting arrangement, from which the entire road on this descent, from the Summit to Panther Creek,

takes its name of the Switch-Back Railroad. At every point where a turn or change in the direction is made, the two tracks (that is, the one descending in one direction, and the other continuing the descent at an angle with the first) come together like the angle at the top of a Y, and unite in one track, running out like the foot of the same letter. This one track, on the foot of the Y, however, has an ascending grade, up which the car is carried by the force of the momentum it has acquired in its downward course. As soon as this momentum is exhausted, of course the car begins to run down the ascent, but instead of running back a little distance up the same it has just before descended, the switch at the fork of the Y is arranged with a spring which adjusts the switch to the track which descends at an angle with the first, so that the car upon its descent from the single track continues on its way down the mountain. And so we go at a most rapid rate, now this way, now that way; the breeze caused by the rapid motion renders it necessary for us to keep hold of our hats, bonnets and all other matters liable to be carried away, now dashing round a curve at what seems a frightful speed, and now resting a moment as the switch-back changes our course, and again away with the speed of the wind, we reach the bottom of the valley. Here we have leisure to rest ourselves and examine the coal breakers before commencing our ascent. The grade of the track through this valley is 60 feet to the mile; we pass by a number of coal-breakers, tunnels and mining villages. You will notice here the rubbish has been deposited by successive loads, until nearly a hundred artificial hills have been made, radiating in all directions from the mines. These hills overtop the highest trees; one of them, you will notice, has a reddish hue; it has been on fire for over twenty years, and has every prospect of burning until the end of time. Visitors are permitted to enter the mines, and are accommodated with a guide, but as our time is limited, be will be unable to satisfy our curiosity.[146]

The only other description of any detail of these switches is found in the *History of Lehigh and Carbon Counties* by Mathews and Hungerford, most likely lifted from the MS Henry description.

These well-known switches were not long in use. By 1860 the Springvale switches were gone, and the Jamestown switches were torn up circa 1862.[147]

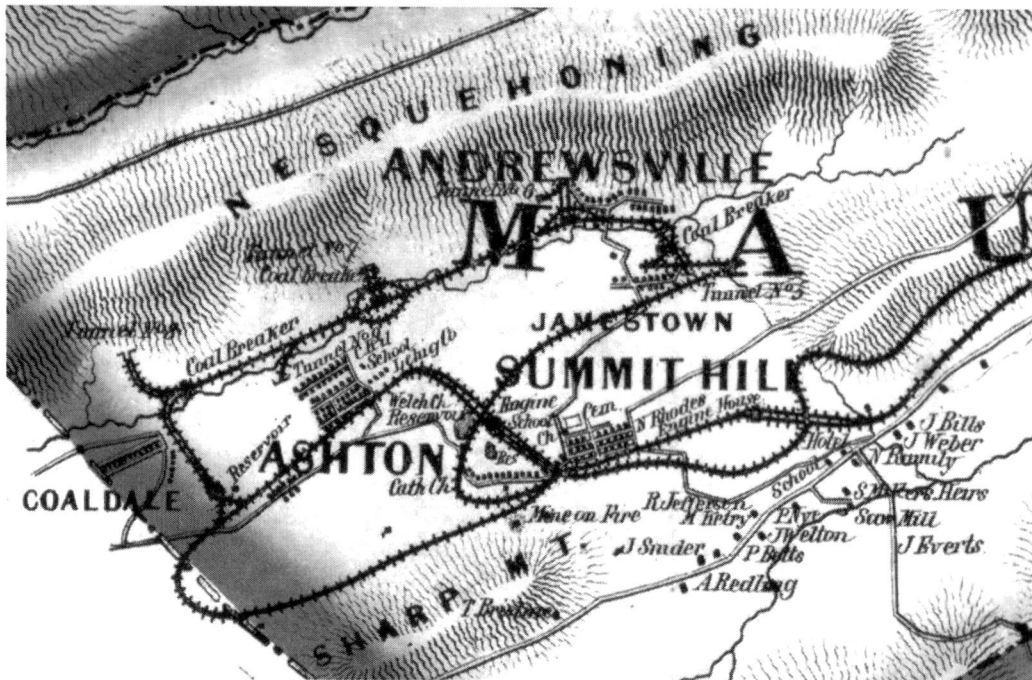

This section of an 1860 map shows that the Springvale switch-backs have been replaced with a long curving track. Adapted from "Map of the Counties of Monroe and Carbon Pennsylvania." Published by Loomis Way & Palmer, 1860

Devotees of the Switchback Railroad sometimes state that the switches were used for braking or slowing the cars. This was true, but in an indirect way. These switches permitted the use of shallow grades with longer track runs, rather than a more direct and steeper grade of track. The longer run of track meant more friction, and therefore less of a braking problem. The use of these switches was simply to change the direction of the car, automatically, and thus stretch out the descent over a grade than was not as steep as otherwise. Newspaper accounts of trips into the Panther Creek Valley indicate that brakemen were used on the trips.[148]

These switches were also used on the Hacklebernie Gravity railroad, constructed in 1854 to connect the LC&N's Hacklebernie Tunnel with the Mauch Chunk and Summit Hill Gravity Railroad.

These switches were in use for only a relatively short period of time. Perhaps better braking mechanisms dispensed with the need for them.

Miners posing before going to work in one of the Panther Valley mine tunnels.

Slope No. 2

BESIDES THE CONSTRUCTION of the Second Return Backtrack, the year 1850 saw the implementation of another major change to the valley system. This was the opening of Slope No. 2 on the northwest side of the abandoned Old Quarry. This new slope was driven to gain access to the south dip of the saddle-shaped mammoth vein as it dropped downward into Panther Valley.

Slope No. 2 was driven by George Belford and Richard Sharpe, who were also contracted to construct a railroad yard and car stands at the Summit, east of the Old Quarry and Summit mines.[149] This work was completed before January 1, 1851.[150] Eventually an extensive marshaling yard, located at the present site of Ludlow Park in Summit Hill, was built for storing and shunting loaded and empty cars between the various mines and the coal breaker.

Panther Valley Summary Timeline: 1851

➢ January 1, 1851: Robert H. Sayre, the LC&N's on-site engineer in the Panther Valley, begins keeping a personal diary.

➢ Early 1851: Panther Creek Inclined Plane No. 3, aka Sharp Mountain Plane, completed along with railroad to service Slope No. 2.

➢ Early 1851: Completion of coal breaker for Slope No. 2.

➢ During 1851 State geologist Henry Darwin Rogers visited and reported on the operations of the LC&N in the Panther Creek Valley.

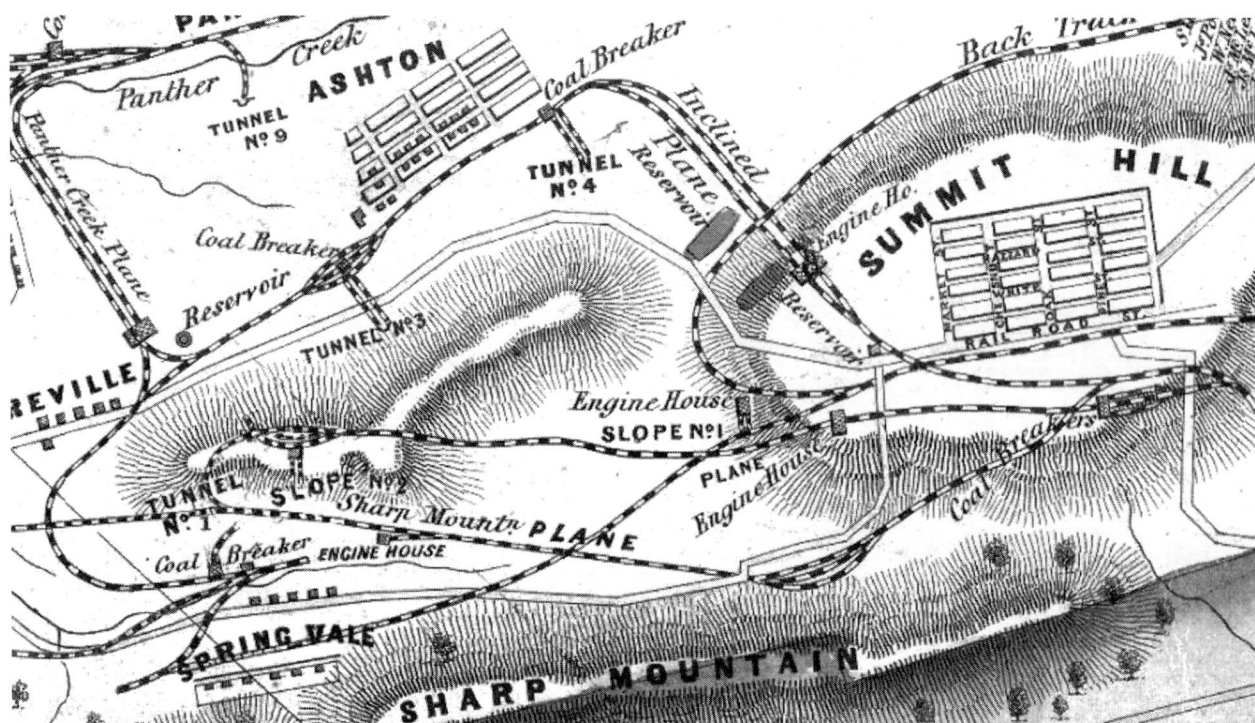

This section of the 1854 Nunan map shows Slope No. 2, driven in 1851, located near Tunnel No. 1 on the west side of the Old Quarry. Cars loaded with coal from this new slope were hauled to the Summit on the Sharp Mountain inclined plane.

The Sharp Mountain Inclined Plane

As part of their contract Belford and Sharpe also constructed a new inclined plane 3000 feet long, extending from the Springvale area to the Summit of Sharp Mountain, behind the Summit Mines. This plane came to be known as the Sharp Mountain inclined plane, or sometimes as Panther Creek Inclined Plane No. 3. These changes, including breaking and screening fixtures for Slope No. 2 were completed and in operation by April of 1851.[151] Similar in design to Panther Creek Plane No. 1, this inclined plane had the engine house located at a midpoint on the plane, rather than at the head of the plane.

The new railroad and inclined plane were built to service Slope No. 2. Empty coal cars were directed to Slope No. 2 from the marshaling yards in Summit Hill. They coasted across a trestle spanning the abandoned Old Quarry to Slope No. 2. Loaded cars then coasted to the foot of the Sharp Mountain inclined plane, where they were raised to the top of the mountain and drifted by gravity to the coal breaker at Summit Hill.

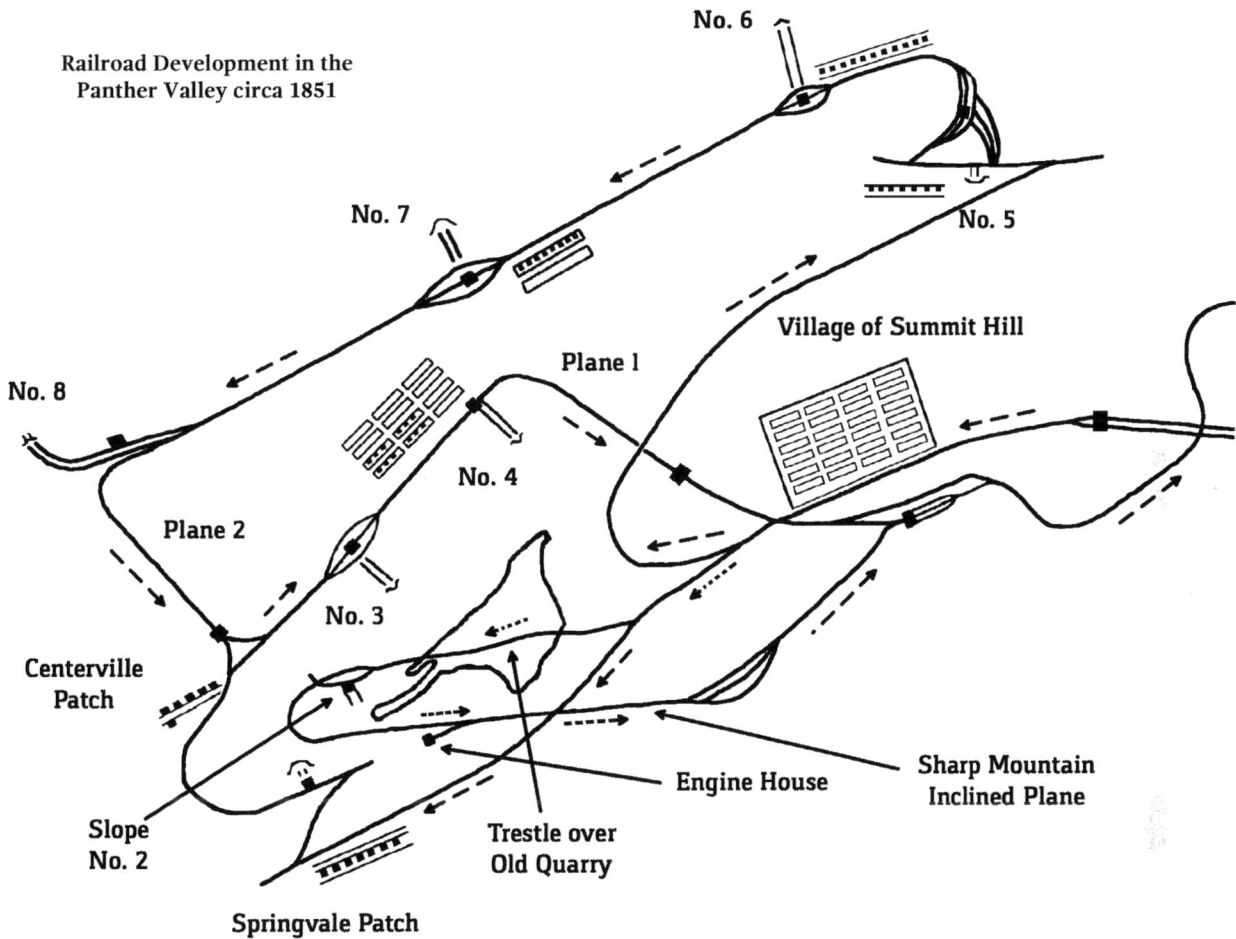

Railroad Development in the
Panther Valley circa 1851

Panther Valley Railroad Development circa 1851. This map depicts the railroads in the Panther Valley after the old quarry had been abandoned and a trestle had been constructed to span the quarry. Also visible is the Sharp Mountain Inclined plane, which was constructed to gain access to Slope No. 2. This slope was located on the northwestern side of the old quarry and attacked the south dip of the mammoth vein. The Sharp Mountain inclined plane would also be used for raising coal mined at Foster's Tunnel to the summit of Sharp Mountain. Map adapted by the author from the 1854 Philip Nunan Map and other sources

Biographical Digression: Richard Sharpe (1813-1895)

RICHARD SHARPE immigrated to America with his family at the age of 13, settling in Wilkes-Barre. He arrived in Summit Hill in 1838, where he began his apprenticeship in the coal mining business employed as bookkeeper by James Broderick and George Davis, who held a mining contract at the summit. Sharpe, like many of his acquaintances, was an active member of St. Mark's Episcopal Church in Mauch Chunk, serving as a vestryman from 1844 to 1850.

Richard Sharpe
Luzerne County Historical Society

In 1845 Richard Sharpe joined the contracting firm of Ira Cortright, George Belford, John Leisenring and Francis Weiss. These men held LC&N contracts for mining at the Summit. In 1847 Sharpe married Sally Patterson, sister to Nathan Patterson, the LC&N Mine Agent at Summit Hill.[152]

In September of 1850 George Belford and Richard Sharpe also teamed up to take a contract rebuilding dams on the Lehigh Navigation after they were destroyed by a freshet.[153]

Sharpe was yet another member of the firm that formed the Council Ridge Colliery and the village of Eckley in the 1850s. Sharpe and his family remained at Eckley until 1874, when they moved to Wilkes-Barre.

Biographical Digression: Merit Abbott (1806-1874)

MERIT ABBOTT and family were among the earliest settlers in Mauch Chunk, arriving in 1820. According to some sources, his mother was the first interment in the Upper Mauch Chunk cemetery.[154]

In 1837 the LC&N hired Abbott, a young engineer with experience in the installation of machinery in large mills, to be responsible for installing "engines at the mines, and any other work the Superintendent may direct," at a yearly salary of $700. That year Abbott moved to Summit Hill and began his work for the LC&N in earnest.[155]

In 1851, seeking further opportunity, he partnered with Alexander Lockhart to purchase a lot in Summit Hill and erect a foundry.[156] This foundry, located as it was in the heart of the operations of the Lehigh Coal and Navigation Company, received most if not all the machinery contracts for the LC&N up to 1872, when the LC&N shops were moved from Summit Hill down into the valley near the patch town of Ashton. Robert Heysham Sayre, who had relocated sometime prior to 1851, spent much of his working time visiting the foundry to check on work in progress.

The partnership between Merit and Lockhart was dissolved in the Spring of 1851; Abbott continued to run the business himself. In 1854 Abbott partnered with Andrew J. Winterstein (aka Wintersteen) to purchase another lot, upon which the men erected a town hall, which was used for community gatherings, including dances and plays. Following the outbreak of the Civil War the building was used as a headquarters for the Carbon Guards, a military company organized by Winterstein. Following the Civil War, the building was used as a armory by the Pennsylvania National Guard.[157]

The "Bastille" building in Summit Hill was constructed ca 1854 by Merit Abbott and A.J. Winterstein, and was used for a town hall. It later became the home of the Carbon Guards, a military company organized by Winterstein.

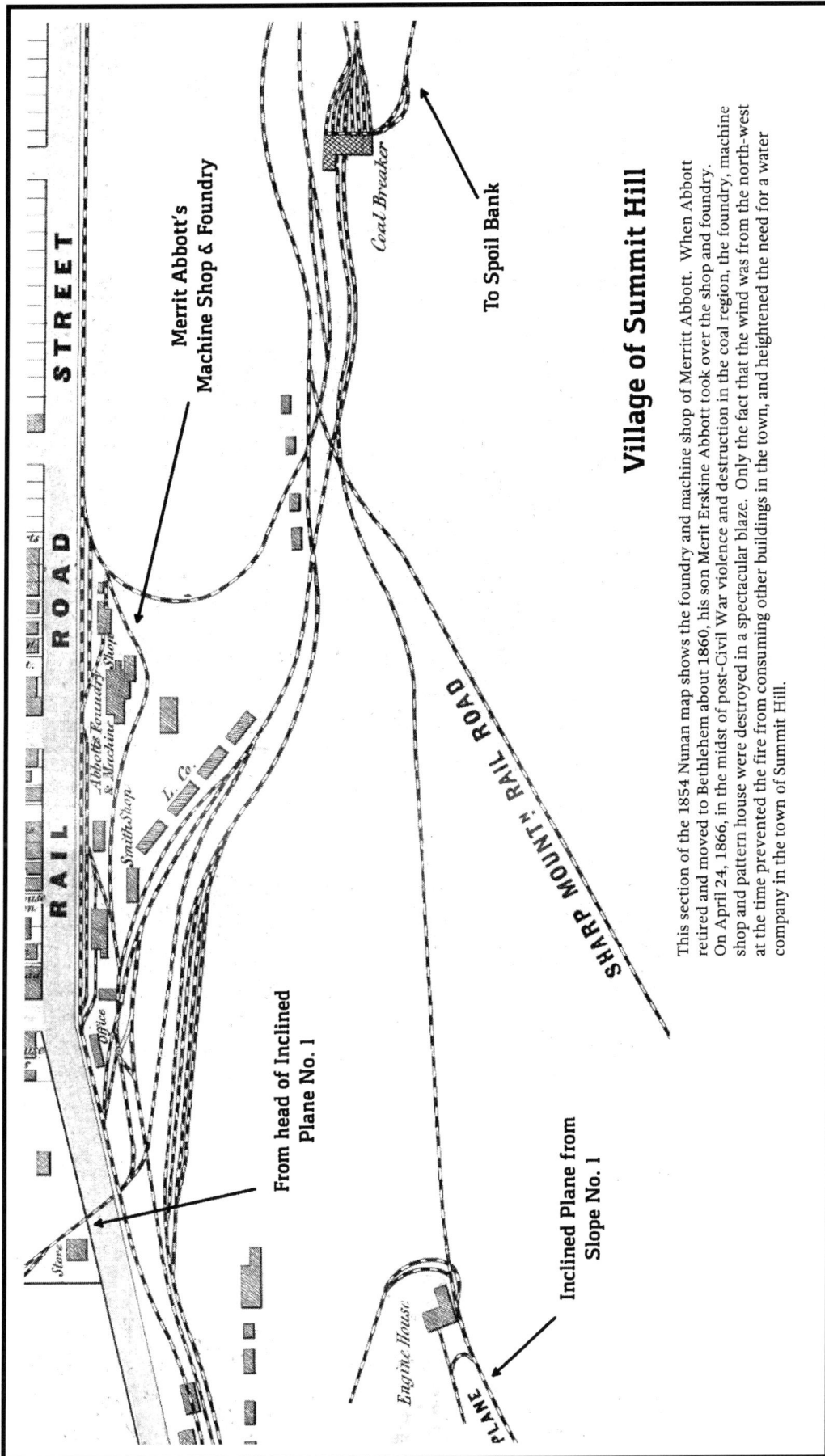

Village of Summit Hill

This section of the 1854 Nunan map shows the foundry and machine shop of Merritt Abbott. When Abbott retired and moved to Bethlehem about 1860, his son Merit Erskine Abbott took over the shop and foundry. On April 24, 1866, in the midst of post-Civil War violence and destruction in the coal region, the foundry, machine shop and pattern house were destroyed in a spectacular blaze. Only the fact that the wind was from the north-west at the time prevented the fire from consuming other buildings in the town, and heightened the need for a water company in the town of Summit Hill.

Merit Abbott and A.J. Winterstein also partnered in coal mining, accepting a contract to mine coal from Slopes 1 and 2 for the years 1855 through 1860.[158] In 1865 Merit Abbott retired and moved to Bethlehem.[159] Abbott was well known in the anthracite industry, travelling to Europe with Asa Packer in 1865.[160] In His Last Will and Testament he bequeathed a valuable collection of minerals and case to John Leisenring, Jr., his life-long friend.[161]

Merit's son, Robert Adams Abbott, followed in his father's footsteps, taking contracts in and around the Panther Valley.

Biographical Digression: Andrew Jackson Wintersteen (NA-1863)

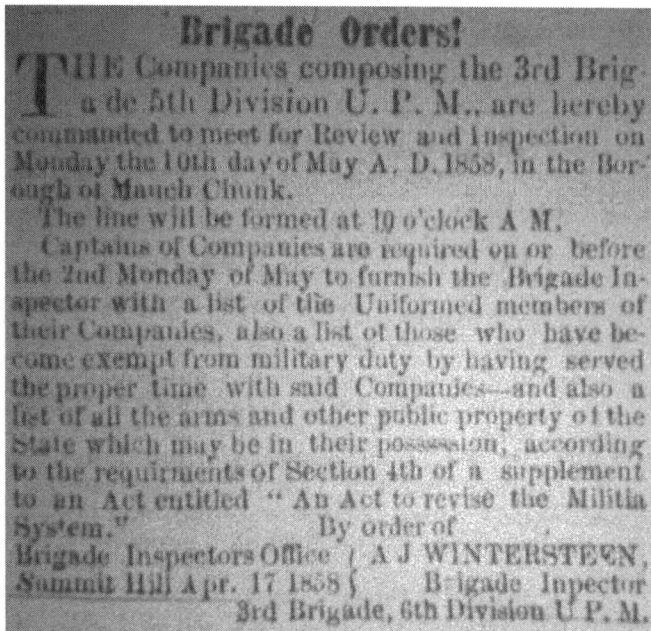

From the Mauch Chunk Gazette, 29 Apr 1858, DMK

ANDREW J. WINTERSTEIN (also sp. Wintersteen) was another rather unknown individual who lived and worked at the summit of Sharp Mountain, and in the Panther Valley. In 1847 Winterstein, known generally as "Jackson," operated a line of passenger cars between Summit Hill and Mauch Chunk on the LC&N's old gravity railroad.[162] "Jackson" married Mary Taylor McConnell, the daughter of LC&N colliery physician Benjamin Rush McConnell, on December 31, 1850.[163]

The following year Jackson organized the Carbon Guards, a Summit Hill military company with Daniel Dingman Brodhead as Captain, Eli Taylor Conner as 1st Lieutenant, Jackson himself as 2nd Lieutenant, Robert A. Abbott as second 2nd Lt, and John W. Pryor as Orderly Sergeant. Besides the 4 officers, an inspection in August of 1851 counted 32 non-commissioned and privates. By 1858 Jackson was Captain of the Company.[164]

In 1860, following the death of Dr. McConnell's widow, Jackson applied to the LC&N for permission to move, with his family, into the home occupied by Mrs. McConnell,

> and makes application to have the house enlarged so as to accommodate both families, Mrs. McConnell being his wife's mother, the cost of the proposed enlargement is estimated at $350, for which he is willing to pay such additional rent as is usually assessed upon similar improvements. And On Motion, Resolved that the application be agreed to.[165]

Jackson was one of a group of men, praised by LC&N Superintendent and Engineer John Leisenring, for service during the reconstruction of the company's navigation system following the disastrous flood of June 1862.[166]

In 1862, while traveling the gravity railroad from Summit Hill to Mauch Chunk, the car he was traveling in with several other men, collided with a coal car, severely bruising Jackson and the other men, although not critically. Jackson died in January of 1863, of smallpox.[167]

66

Biographical Digression: Robert Adams Abbott (1832-1902)

ROBERT A. ABBOTT was one of four children born to Merit Abbott. At 19 years of age he was part of the Carbon Guards at Summit Hill.[168] In 1859, at the age of 27 he partnered with Hugh L. Davis to take his first mining contract, a three-year agreement to mine and deliver coal from valley Tunnel No. 8.[169] In August of 1862 Abbott mustered into Civil War operations as Captain with Company G, 132nd Pennsylvania Infantry. His civil war service was short-lived, however. A month later, at the battle of Antietam, his lower jaw was shot away by a Confederate Minnie ball. In January of 1863 Abbott was discharged at Washington, DC. Abbott returned to the valley and continued to take mining contracts and in 1865 was still living in and doing business in and around Summit Hill. Sometime before 1870 he retired from the mining business and moved to Bethlehem, Pa.[170]

Abbott died of shock in Bethlehem in 1902 following the death of two grandchildren who died of scarlet fever.[171]

Robert Adams Abbott, one of the four children of Merit Abbott. Findagrave.com

NOTICE

THE subscribers have formed a Co-Part-nership under the name and firm of Chapman & Abbot, to carry on the Lumber business on Summit Hill.
L. F. CHAPMAN,
R. A. ABBOTT.

Abbott partnered with many individuals, including Lansford Foster Chapman, who was later killed in Civil War action. *Mauch Chunk Gazette* 14 Jul 1859

Biographical Digression: George Hyer Davis (1806-1880)

GEORGE H DAVIS was another early resident of Mauch Chunk, arriving there in the early 1830s. By 1834 he had moved to Summit Hill, where he married Rosamund, daughter of LC&N contractor Samuel Holland, who had taken some of the earliest contracts at Room Run and Summit Hill. By 1837 Davis was a partner in a contracting firm consisting of Samuel Holland, Alexander Lockhart, James Broderick, James McLean and George Kelso, mining coal at the old quarry on the Summit of Sharp Mountain.[172]

His marriage to Rosamund was short lived. In 1837 she died at Summit Hill of consumption, only 22 years old.[173]

Davis served as postmaster at Summit Hill from 1838 to 1845, and in 1839 married Eliza, daughter of business partner James Broderick. His last contract in the Panther Valley was for mining coal from Tunnel No. 6. By 1850 Davis had retired from the coal mining business and moved to Nesquehoning, where he kept a "Public House." [174]

Biographical Digression: Robert Heysham Sayre (1824-1907)

IT IS NOT KNOWN EXACTLY when Robert Heysham Sayre began work as on-site engineer in the Panther Creek Valley. The LC&N Board of Managers meeting minutes record the fact that both his father, William H. Sayre, and his brother, Francis R. Sayre worked for the LC&N, including their salaries. Interestingly, there is no mention of Robert, which seems to indicate that he was not directly on the LC&N payroll, but rather was hired by Edwin Douglas and received a stipend from Douglas himself. By January 1, 1851, when he began keeping a personal diary, Robert Sayre had already relocated to the Panther Valley.

Robert Heysham Sayre, Mauch Chunk Museum and Cultural Center

Edwin Douglas hired Sayre in 1842, after he had already proven himself as an engineer on the Morris Canal.[175] In 1883 Alfred Mathews and Austin N. Hungerford wrote one of the most accurate histories of Carbon County. However, they also made some mistakes. On page 673 they wrote:

"William H. Sayre, who came here in 1829, was the surveyor and builder of the "back track" on Mount Pisgah, and of the Panther Creek Valley Railroad. "[176]

This statement is not correct, for it was not William Sayre, who surveyed these railroads, but his son, Robert. Although William H. Sayre, Sr., did work for the LC&N, he was a clerk in the Company's Mauch Chunk office. The Sayre family lived in the bottom half of a two-story stone house on the Lehigh Canal towpath just below Mauch Chunk, close to the weighlock, where William Sayre Sr. later became weighmaster. Nathan Patterson, another LC&N employee, lived in the top half.[177] Robert Heysham Sayre married Mary E. Smith, of Brooklyn, Susquehanna County, in April of 1845, the couple relocating to the Panther Valley soon after. By 1851, when he began keeping a diary, he was already living in the Valley. There he served as an engineer under Douglas. Although Sayre developed a close friendship with George Washington Salkeld, another Douglas protégé, whom he referred to as "Washington," his relationship with Douglas, whom he refers to as "Mr. Douglas," remained very formal.[178]

Copies of Sayre's diaries are digitized and available on Lehigh University's website and provide an interesting and unique perspective on Panther Valley life in the 1850s. Sayre meticulously recorded weather observations each day, and a general idea of where he was and what he worked on during his day.

Sayre recorded that on an excessively cold day on Tuesday, January 20, 1852, the thermometer at Summit Hill "stood at" 24 degrees below zero. Sayre also recorded the deaths of people close to him. For instance, on February 25, 1852, Sayre recorded the death of G. Washington's Salkeld's mother, Hannah Hugg Salkeld.

Perhaps Sayre's saddest Panther Valley diary entry concerned the death of two of James McLean's children over the space of a few days. He noted that on August 6, 1851, a clear and pleasant day which he spent making preparations for McLean's children's funeral . . . both buried in one coffin . . .[179]

His diary also reveals that Sayre was a deeply religious man, going to weekly Sunday School, which he taught, and then to church on Sunday afternoon. When he wasn't touring valley operations by daily trips over both the "old" and "new" valley switchbacks, he was usually in his garden, weather permitting. Sayre records that valley residents shared plants, especially vegetables.

Sayre also spent a part of most days at the office, shops and foundry located near the head of Plane No. 1 in Summit Hill. In addition to his responsibilities at the Summit and in the Panther Creek valley, Sayre was also in charge of the machinery and equipment on the Mount Jefferson inclined plane and engine house.

Sayre's diary entries also record that the Panther Valley experienced a severe drought in 1851, which had a tremendous impact on Switch-Back Railroad operations, since the steam engines on the inclined planes required a steady water supply for the boilers.

Sayre didn't remain in the Valley very long. A little over a year after he began making his diary entries, Sayre was tapped to survey the route for a steam powered locomotive railroad along the Lehigh River. However, contrary to popular opinion, Asa Packer did not approach Robert Sayre for the job of locating his railroad. His diaries record that the position of Engineer on the "Mauch Chunk to Easton Railroad" was offered to him by his boss, Edwin Douglas.

On May 2, 1852, a "rather pleasant" Sunday morning, Sayre went to Sunday School and church, and then said goodbye to his "Schollars" (sic). He then moved his family and belongings to Mauch Chunk, while he worked at his new job, a task that it appears he was not completely prepared for.

In 1855 Sayre was appointed LVRR general superintendent, a position he held until 1882. He eventually rose to the position of second vice president of the railroad.[180]

East Bertsch Street in Lansford circa 1887. Courtesy of the National Canal Museum, a program of the Delaware & Lehigh National Heritage Corridor, Easton, PA

Looking west in the Panther Valley circa 1870 at the breaker for coal mine Tunnel No. 8. Constructed in 1858, this breaker stood just to the east of the foot of the Panther Creek inclined plane No. 2 and was replaced in 1873 with a new breaker. From a stereoview by MA Kleckner

Biographical Digression: George Washington Salkeld (1815-1861)

GEORGE W SALKELD, "Washington" to his friends, is another of the many "mystery" men in the history of the Lehigh coal region. To date, no pictures of him have been found, and little has been written about him. Though older than Robert Sayre by almost a decade, the men became good friends following Washington's childhood rescue of Sayre:

> While several small boys were amusing themselves in fishing in the Mauch Chunk Basin, on Friday of last week, one of them, a son of Mr. Wm. H. Sayre, accidentally fell in and immediately sunk to the bottom. The attention of Washington Salkeld . . . was called to the spot by one of the boys saying that Robert was in the water. The instant he discovered the situation of the boy, threw off his hat, plunged to the bottom, and succeeded in rescuing the little sufferer from drowning.[181]

That was just one of Salkeld's heroic rescues. In 1858 Salkeld rescued a deaf and dumb 10-year-old girl who was struck by a Switch-Back tourist car near breaker No. 6 in the Panther Valley. Salkeld carried the girl to her home, but it is not recorded whether she survived the trauma.[182]

George W. was one of the many children of Isaac Salkeld, an early LC&N employee who had worked for White and Hazard at their mill at the Falls of the Schuylkill. According to Mathews and Hungerford, George W. Salkeld invented the Switch-Backs in the Panther Creek Valley. He was also involved in the creation of the Mauch Chunk wire rope factory, along with Douglas and Sayre.[183]

Although little is known Salkeld's later life, in 1851 he was still an assistant engineer for the LC&N. Washington eventually left the company to work at the foundry of his brother, Jacob Hugg Salkeld, who ran Mauch Chunk's Lower Foundry in partnership with Samuel Bradley. For the last ten years of his life, he suffered from consumption; he died in 1861.[184]

Biographical Digression: Henry Darwin Rogers (1808-1866)

Henry Darwin Rogers |Source = [http://www. archive.org/details/popularsciencemo50n-ewy Popular Science Monthly Volume 50] |Date = 1896 [Public Domain]

HENRY D ROGERS, a geologist appointed head of Pennsylvania's First Geological Survey in 1836, visited and reported on Nesquehoning's Room Run mines in 1840. At that time, mining in the Panther Valley was only in the planning stage.

In 1852 as part of the Second Geological Survey, Rogers revisited the Room Run mines at Nesquehoning. The previous year, he examined the LC&N's expanding production facilities in the Panther Valley.   Robert H. Sayre spent some time with the Professor, recording an afternoon spent with him on October 22, 1851:

"Went to Mount Jefferson spring. . . Went around Switch Back engaged part of the afternoon with Professor Rogers." [185]

In his report for the Second Geological Survey, Rogers made general observations of the Valley, as well as specific observations about different mines. For example, he noticed that the tunnels in the valley sloped downward toward the mine opening at a fall of 6 inches to every 100 feet of length, to facilitate water drainage.[186]

Rogers also reported that the cost of raising coal from the valley floor to the summit of Sharp Mountain over the two Panther Creek inclined planes was

. . . about four cents per ton; the lift, about 600 feet, is accomplished by two planes. This includes interest on planes, &c.[187]

Rogers reported that Tunnel No. 8 had a red ash vein of 7 feet in thickness "between the slates" and at that time, it was the only red ash vein worked in the valley. Rogers also reported on the economics of mining at Tunnel No. 8. Coal cost 37 ½ cents (per ton) to mine it, another 12 cents to break and clean it. Hoisting the coal from Tunnel 8 to the summit of Sharp Mountain and "running it" to Mauch Chunk cost 12 ½ cents, with another 12 ½ cents for miscellaneous expenses.

The engine of No. 8 Breaker is 20 horse-power. It hauls the coal up from tunnel-level to Breaker. Other Breakers have usually 10-horse-power engines. The Tunnel No. 8 is 13 feet wide, 8 feet high, has a double track at its mouth, and turn-outs within. The rails in the tunnel are of half-inch iron on wooden sleepers. One mule brings out three loaded cars.[188]

The professor's observations also included transportation of coal in the Valley:

Let us begin at the remotest part of the line, say at Tunnels No. 6 or No. 7 in Panther Creek Valley. The coal-cars, after receiving their freights of coal, previously picked and screened near the mines, convey it, by force of gravity alone, upon a gently-inclined railway track, graded with an inclination of not less than 40 feet to the mile, along the immediate valley of Panther Creek to the foot of Plane No. 2. Here they are coupled into sets of three, and hoisted rapidly by ample stationary power to the summit of the plane.[189]

At the head of Panther Valley inclined plane No. 2, the cars coasted by gravity to the foot of Inclined Plane No. 1. After being hoisted to the summit, cars were combined into trains of no more than sixteen for the gravity ride to Mauch Chunk. After discharging coal into the loading schutes on the Lehigh River, the empty cars were returned to the summit overlooking the Panther Creek Valley, where they began their descent back to the mines on one of the return Switch-Backs, depending upon their destination mine.

Panther Valley Coal Mine Tunnel No. 8, sometime in the 1860s. From a stereopticon slide by Mauch Chunk photographer Joseph Brown.

Panther Valley Summary Timeline: 1852

➤ January 14, 1852: LC&N contracts with Daniel Bertsch to drive Tunnel No. 9.
➤ May 5, 1852: Robert H. Sayre's last day as Panther Valley on-site engineer. He went on to survey the LVRR for Asa Packer.

The LC&N's Return to Prosperity

WITH THE COMPLETION of the valley railroad, Slope No. 2 and the Sharp Mountain Inclined Plane, the LC&N was poised for a dramatic rise in coal production. Over the next few years production increased from 330,447 tons in 1850, to 393,353 tons in 1851 and 429,786 tons in 1852.

LC&N managers did not rejoice in the increased production, but rather complained that even greater output, as permitted by facilities in the Panther Valley, was limited by "the boating facilities within the control of the producers." [190]

Regardless of the LC&N managers gloomy view, the increased coal production boosted LC&N income, assisting it in its return to prosperity. By 1852 the company had reinstated its dividend and interest payments and had begun the process of debt reduction. In 1852 the earnings per share of common stock was a healthy 14.3 percent of share value, growing to 21 percent in 1853 and leaping to an astounding 30.2 percent in 1854.[191]

Still Another Tunnel

TO RAISE PANTHER VALLEY coal production even further, on January 14 of 1852 the LC&N authorized a contract with Daniel Bertsch to drive Tunnel No. 9 into the south side of the Panther Valley, 10 feet wide by 8 feet high.[192]

Tunnel No. 9 proved to be one of the most difficult Valley projects. By the end of 1853, after tunneling 195 yards at a cost of $9,807.81

Office of the Lehigh Coal and Navigation Company.

MAUCH CHUNK, DEC. 12, 1851.

To Contractors.

PROPOSALS will be received at this office and at the Company's office at Summit Hill, until the first day of January next, for driving a Tunnel about seven hundred yards in length, on the south side of Panther Creek Valley.

For Specifications and blank propositions apply at this office, or to Rob't H. Sayre, resident Engineer at Summit Hill.

E. A. DOUGLAS,
Sup't. and Engineer.

Carbon County Gazette, 18 Dec 1851, DML

"the rock suddenly dipped down below the bottom of the tunnel, leaving a bed of quicksand to contend with. After several attempts to secure it with timber, it was given up as impracticable, without incurring a large and unjustifiable expense, and, as a final resort, it was concluded to make an open cut, about 150 feet in length, and 70 feet in depth, which will require three or four months to complete. "[193]

Determined to press onward toward the valley's major coal seam, the new tunnel reached the mammoth vein on Christmas Day 1857 after being driven 2,283 feet. In late April of the following year the breaker for Tunnel No. 9 was completed and used for the first time.[194]

Coal was extracted from this mine until June 22, 1972. A preservation group took possession of the tunnel in 1992. Restoration was started in 1995 and in 2002 tours were started.[195]

[Left] Coal Mine Tunnel No. 9 sometime in the 1890s. From a stereoview by Mauch Chunk photographer James Zellner.

Breaker for Panther Valley Coal Mine Tunnel No. 9. This breaker was constructed in 1876 and torn down in 1909 and was known as the "Dry Breaker." Bob Gormley

Panther Valley Summary Timeline: 1853-54

➢ November 1853: Tunnel No. 2 breaker and railroad under contract.
➢ During 1854: A backtrack leading from Springvale to Tunnel No. 2 and a new inclined plane at Tunnel No. 2 in progress. Work temporarily halted due to scarcity of labor.

This "Exterior View of the Coal Mines" shows the Old Quarry, along with abandoned gangways, as it appeared in 1853. The Summit Hill coal breaker is visible in the distance. After the quarry was abandoned, the gangways served to provide light and ventilation to the underground mines leading from the valley below. "The Coal-Beds of Pennsylvania," *Illustrated News*, 15 Jan 1854, 36

Reviving the Foster's Tunnel and Railroad

THE LC&N HAD AWARDED the first contract to drive Panther Valley Tunnel No. 2 to Asa Lansford Foster and Robert Q. Butler in January of 1846. Little work, if any, was done and the tunnel produced no coal at that time.

In October of 1847 the LC&N ordered the construction of a railroad from Tunnel No. 2 to the foot of Panther Creek plane No. 2. However, this railroad was never built. It wasn't until November of 1853 that a railroad and all machinery necessary to remove coal from Tunnel No. 2, located south of the present site of the borough of Coaldale, was put under contract.[196]

It is difficult to fathom the reasoning behind the "as-built" Foster's tunnel railroad. Instead of constructing a railroad from Tunnel No. 2 to the foot of inclined plane No. 2, as originally planned, the company built a separate railroad, including an additional inclined plane as well as a return track that only serviced Tunnel No. 2. This was certainly a more expensive design and significantly raised the cost of mining at this tunnel.

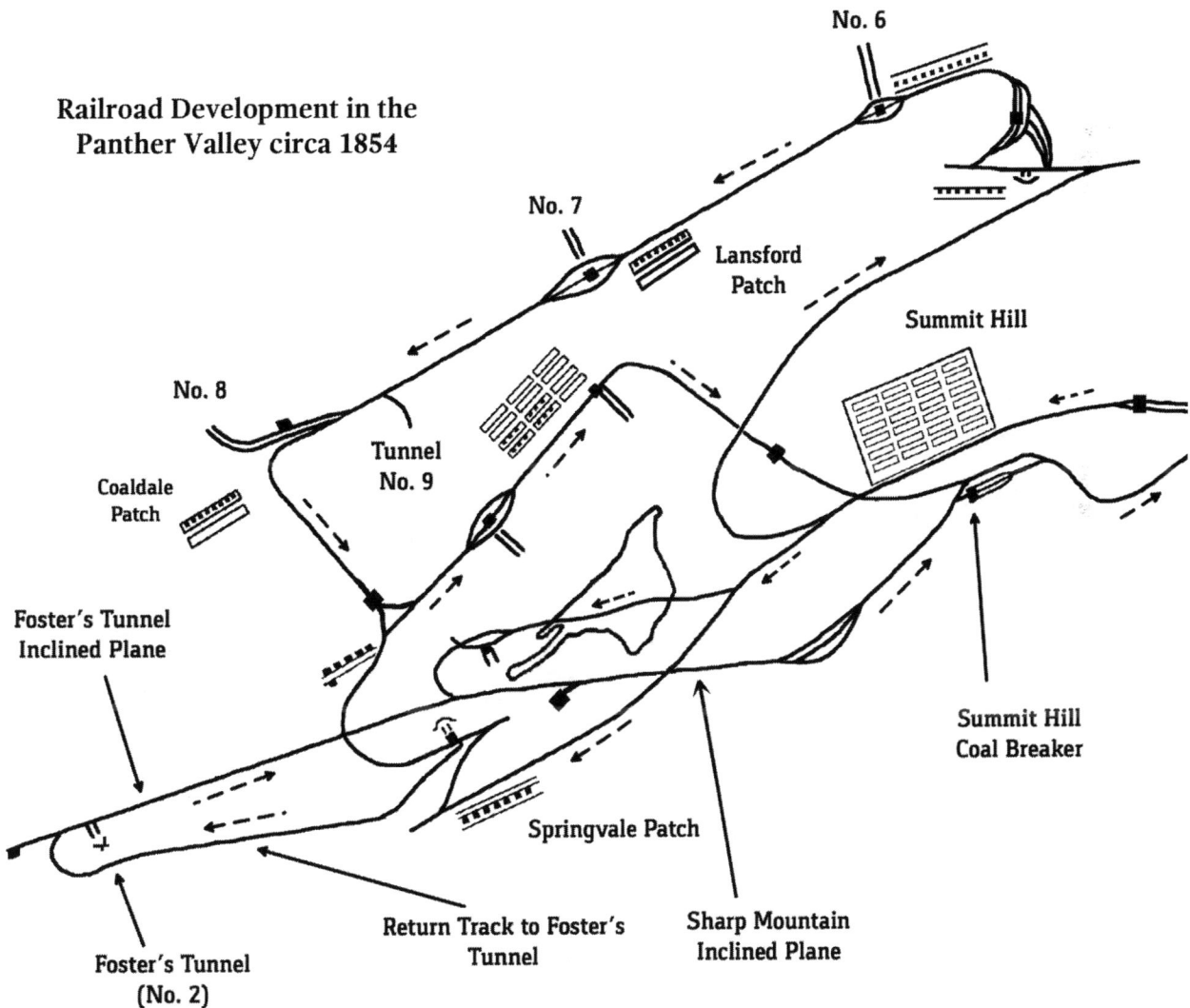

Railroad development in the Panther Valley circa 1854 after an inclined plane and backtrack had been constructed to service Tunnel No. 2, The plane and backtrack remained in service less than 10 years. Map adapted by the author from the 1854 Philip Nunan Map

By the end of 1854 contractors had built a backtrack leading from Springvale to Tunnel No. 2; laid track on the new inclined plane and started construction of necessary colliery support buildings. Although almost $29,000 had already been spent, completion of the work was postponed due to scarcity of labor and the high wages resulting.[197] An interesting feature of the Foster's Tunnel plane was that the engine house was located at the foot of the plane.

As with slope No. 2, Foster's Tunnel utilized its own inclined plane for hoisting coal up the mountainside. The Foster's Tunnel inclined plane led from the mouth of Tunnel No. 2 to the foot of the Sharp Mountain inclined plane. Thus, coal coming out of the tunnel was hauled to the summit by two planes in succession.

The work at Foster's Tunnel was finally completed in September of 1855, although, due to a lack of demand for coal, the facility was not put into operation. Coal from Foster's Tunnel was not mined until 1857 when 10,015 tons of coal were removed from this tunnel. Production declined from this point until the year 1859 when only 71 tons were removed from the mine.[198]

Journey to the Promised Land

THE LAST PANTHER CREEK VALLEY contract awarded to Asa Lansford Foster was made in December of 1849 for the construction of a section of the Panther Creek Railroad. For an unknown reason, Foster took no more valley mining contracts, instead had bookkeeping duties for Daniel Bertsch to provide him with an income.

Looking East at the plane for the Tunnel No. 8 coal breaker from a stereoview by M.A. Kleckner, circa 1870. This breaker was placed in service in 1857 and abandoned in 1873. The slate-pickers "shanty" stands to the right of the breaker and in the far distance the breaker for Tunnel No. 7 is visible. Ray Holland

The firm consisting of George Belford, Richard Sharpe, John Leisenring, Ira Cortright and Francis Weiss received a contract to mine coal from the summit mines as well as Slope No. 1 for the years 1848 and 1849.[199] This firm, known as Belford, Sharpe, and Company, continued to work the summit mines and slope No. 1 through 1854, and probably received the mining contract for Slope No. 2. Although various members of this concern were able to win contracts for construction of railroads within the valley, these men rarely captured mining contracts down in the Valley proper.

Perhaps because of this, the group looked for greener pastures elsewhere.

In 1853 Asa Lansford Foster steered these men to a site in Luzerne County where he had previously observed coal "signs" in the company of Isaac Chapman, an early surveyor who had also located coal at Room Run. These men confirmed significant coal deposits at the eastern end of the Black Creek coal basin in Denison Township.[200]

In 1854 they organized a new company to exploit Foster's Luzerne County discoveries. This firm was known as Sharpe, Leisenring and Company and consisted of Asa Lansford Foster, Richard Sharpe, John Leisenring, Jr., George Belford, Francis Weiss and William Reed, a nephew of Asa Lansford Foster.

William Reed, 1819-1884, was an LC&N clerk who was part of group that formed the Council Ridge Colliery in 1854. Reed was a nephew of Asa Lansford Foster, and was married to Elizabeth Kent Sayre, a sister of Robert Heysham Sayre

Dissolution of Partnership.

THE Copartnership heretofore existing between the Subscribers, under the Firm of SHARPE, LEISENRING & CO., is this day (May 15th, 1860,) DISSOLVED by mutual consent, John Leisenring retiring.

The Accounts of the late firm will be settled by the remaining Partners, who will continue the business of MINING and SELLING COAL from the Council Ridge Colliery under the firm of SHARPE, WEISS & CO.

GEORGE BELFORD, JOHN LEISENRING,
RICHARD SHARPE, FRANCIS WEISS,
Eckley, May 24—6t WILLIAM REED,

Mauch Chunk Gazette, 24 May 1860, DML

One Panther Valley partner who did not take advantage of the new opportunity was Ira Cortright. Cortright's final contract within the Panther Valley was to mine coal from Tunnel No. 8. After completing the contract in early 1857, he moved to South Bethlehem, where he died in 1870.[201]

Sharpe and Company started what was initially called the Council Ridge Colliery. The decision was a gamble, but it paid off big for most of them, as many of the partners became very wealthy as a result. Coal production from the Council Ridge Colliery began as early as 1855, leading to the formation of a town initially called Fillmore, but later known as Eckley. In the Spring of 1855, when Asa Lansford Foster moved from the Panther Valley to Fillmore, there were 38 families already located there.

New Faces and Old Faces

AFTER THE COUNCIL RIDGE CONSORTIUM left the valley a new group of men formed a valley partnership known as Abbott, Sharpe and Company. These men were Merit Abbott, Andrew Jackson Wintersteen and William Sharpe. These men held the mining contracts at the summit until the

LC&N abolished the use of contractors in 1865.[202]

Other contractors left the valley in 1854, creating opportunities for new men in the valley. George Kline and Thomas Philips received the contract to mine coal at Tunnel No. 2.[203] Other new contractors were men named Knowles, Van Horn, Long and Fellows.

One of the few men to remain in the valley was Daniel Bertsch, who continued to receive the mining contracts at Tunnel No. 4. James McLean also remained in the valley, and mined coal at Tunnels No. 5 and 6.

The LC&N was able to get some financial remuneration from the change in the faces:

> Both of the last-mentioned contractors are now entirely out of business in Panther Creek Valley, or the neighborhood. They each own a certain number of dwelling houses built near the mines for the accommodation of miners. They are in want of money to pay off their debts and are anxious to sell these houses. It is believed they will sell them at rates which will yield the Company some 12 per cent per annum over and above all expenses. The committee suggest to the Board the propriety of purchasing these houses as the investment will pay well, and a measure of relief will at the same time be thereby extended to parties who have done good service to the Company.[204]

Double Tracks and T Rails

AS BUILT, Panther Creek planes No. 1 and 2 were single tracked. In 1854 they were working almost to capacity, leading Edwin Douglas to complain that:

> when an accident happens, whether from breaking of a rope, or from cars getting off the track, the interruption is felt throughout the whole line of works.[205]

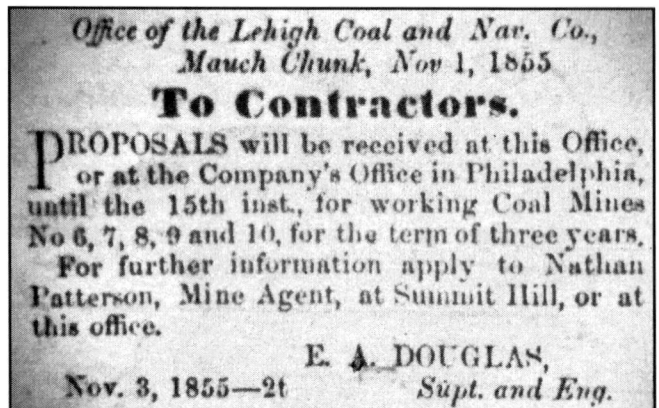

Office of the Lehigh Coal and Nav. Co.,
Mauch Chunk, Nov 1, 1855

To Contractors.

PROPOSALS will be received at this Office, or at the Company's Office in Philadelphia, until the 15th inst., for working Coal Mines No 6, 7, 8, 9 and 10, for the term of three years. For further information apply to Nathan Patterson, Mine Agent, at Summit Hill, or at this office.

E. A. DOUGLAS,
Nov. 3, 1855—2t   *Supt. and Eng.*

Carbon Democrat, **10 Nov 1855, DML**

There was also the inefficiency of having to wait for the safety car to make a complete round trip up and down the inclined plane before another trip of loaded cars could be hoisted.

Douglas suggested that this "evil" could be remedied by double tracking the inclines. That way, if an accident occurred on one side, the engine for that incline could be "thrown out of gear, and the other put in gear in a few minutes." Since the planes were already graded to such a width that would permit the addition of another track, the estimate of the improvement was about $7,000 for each of the planes.[206]

By December of 1855 the strap iron for the additional track had been procured, although it had not been laid. By the open of the season of 1857 the second track was laid, but with T-rail instead of strap iron. Eventually these planes would operate in a manner like Pisgah and Jefferson, that is, as one safety car ascended the plane, another descended on the opposite track.[207]

Panther Valley Summary Timeline: 1855

- ➤ May 1855: George Kline awarded 5 year mining contract Tunnel No. 2.
- ➤ September 1855: Foster's tunnel railroad and colliery completed but not put into operation due to lack of demand for coal.
- ➤ Engines and machinery procured to drive Slope No. 3 in Tunnel No. 6.
- ➤ By end of 1855 Tunnel No. 9 was driven a total of 1119 feet.

This photo of Panther Valley coal breaker No. 8, taken from a stereoview, was part of MA Kleckner's "Trip Around the Switchback" series which was shot in the early 1870s. Ray Holland

Panther Valley Summary Timeline: 1856 & 1857

- ➤ 1856: Daniel Bertsch awarded 3-year mining contract for Tunnel No. 4.
- ➤ 1856: James McLean & Jonathan Simpson ditto 3-year for Tunnels No. 5 & 6.
- ➤ 1856: Knowles, Fellows & Nathan Van Horn 3-year contract for No. 7.
- ➤ 1856: Ira Cortright 3-year mining contract for Tunnel No. 8.
- ➤ 1856: Superstructure on one side of Planes No. 1 and 2 relaid with T rail.
- ➤ 1856: Slope No. 3 within Tunnel No. 6 completed.
- ➤ 1856: Trial slope sunk at Dry Hollow, west of the Springvale Tunnel.
- ➤ 1857: Overproduction of coal plagued the market.
- ➤ 1857: Lehigh River high water interfered with canal transport of coal.
- ➤ 1857: First year coal (10,015 tons) mined from "Foster'" Tunnel.
- ➤ 1857: Official start of the nationwide "Panic of 1857."
- ➤ 1857: Tunnel No. 9 reached the Mammoth Vein on December 25.

Replacement of Strap Iron with T-Rails

THE ORIGINAL SECTIONS of the Panther Creek Railroad were laid with wooden rails and strap iron, both of which deteriorated over time, requiring frequent replacement. It wasn't until the mid 1850s that the LC&N began replacing the original material on all of its railroads with T rails. This work was also pursued with vigor in the Panther Creek Valley, the work being substantially completed by 1858.[208]

The Panic of 1857

STUDIES OF PAST economic downturns in the United States reveal not just one but a variety of causes for these recessions. While the early part of the decade of the 1850s saw rising prosperity across the country, including the coal regions, much of this prosperity has been attributed to a rising US money supply, stimulated by large amounts of gold mined in the western United States. The increased money supply not only stimulated investment, it also stimulated speculation.

The availability of more money for investment, as well as the healthy financial returns from coal sales earlier in the decade, stimulated even greater production among the various coal companies, and the entry of new operators. As might be expected, this resulted in production of coal beyond what the market could absorb, and threatened the prosperity of all the coal producers, including the LC&N. These events impacted coal prices as early as the summer of 1857.

In July of 1857 the *Mauch Chunk Gazette* noted that Schuylkill region coal operators had been shipping coal at prices below the cost of production. A month later the newspaper reported that prices obtained for coal were "ruinously low." [209]

By September of 1857 these events finally reached crisis levels causing the "official" start of a panic, leading to bank runs and the failure of financial firms. The panic caused "suspensions" of various banks and financial institutions, including the Bank of Pennsylvania. In late September

> the Mauch Chunk Bank joined in the general suspension of specie payment. This was rather unexpected to many of our citizens, as no one ever doubted the soundness of the institution. [210]

Specie payment referred to the payment of financial liabilities with gold or silver, rather than with paper notes.

The suspension of the Mauch Chunk Bank did not last very long. On February 4, 1858, the bank resumed specie payments on all its liabilities.[211] However, the economic downturn caused by the Panic of 1857 would not be completely overcome until the Civil War.

While the mines of the LC&N fared somewhat better than those of the Schuylkill region the LC&N President noted, in the Annual Report for the year 1858

> The past year was one of languor and of depression in every department of business and of productive industry. The coal interest could not fail to participate in the general prostration.[212]

The LC&N, recognizing the impact to the Company from coal overproduction, survived the financial panic by ensuring that the coal production of the company would find markets. This was done by large cuts in the canal tolls for coal, and

> the most rigid economy in the expenditures, and by limiting outlays to what was necessary for the preservation of the Company's property, and for the promotion of their business.[213]

Although not explicitly stated, this meant cutting wages, and would result in severe consequences.

80

Panther Valley Summary Timeline: 1858

➢ April 1858. Breaker for Tunnel No. 9 completed.
➢ April 1858: Property of Daniel Bertsch destroyed by fire.

Labor Problems in the Valley and on the Summit

IN EARLY APRIL of 1858 the store, warehouse and office of mining contractor Daniel Bertsch were destroyed by fire, with an uninsured loss of $10,000. Mauch Chunk newspapers stated:

> It was undoubtedly the work of an incendiary, and we sincerely hope that the rascal may be discovered, and receive the punishment he so richly deserves. Mr. Bertsch is a gentleman of wealth, and this calamity will not affect him seriously. His business will go on as usual.[214]

Threats were also made on the property of other valley contractors.

A few days after Bertsch's property was torched, a notice was nailed to the door of Nathan Patterson, the LC&N mine agent, that his property would also be incinerated. Shortly after that, four men were observed approaching the coal breakers operated by James McLean at Tunnels 5 and 6 with combustible materials. Shots were fired at the men, but they escaped.[215]

The LC&N responded to the labor unrest, authorizing Superintendent and Engineer Edwin Douglas •

> . . . to appropriate any sum not exceeding $300, in such manner as he may deem most advisable, in aid of the civil authorities to promote the peace, and protect the property of the Company from lawless attacks.[216]

Nathan Patterson (1803-1882) was the LC&N's mine agent at Summit Hill and in the Panther Creek Valley in the mid 1800s. His sister Sally was married to Richard Sharpe. *A History of the Sabbath School of The First Presbyterian Church Summit Hill, Carbon County Pennsylvania, and A Narrative of the Diamond Jubilee,* 55

The Carbon Guards

AS A RESULT OF THESE ACTIONS, the Carbon Guards were activated, under the command of Captain Andrew Jackson Wintersteen, with between 60 to 70 individuals prepared for any "emergency." [217]

Actions taken seemed to have solved the problem, at least temporarily.

> Order has been fully restored at Summit Hill   The re-organization of the Carbon Guard, under Capt. Wintersteen has had a very good effect. Some of the most troublesome have left the place, and others, probably better disposed, have been employed.[218]

81

Although some sources on Carbon County history peg the formation of the Carbon Guards in 1854, Robert Sayre observed the Guards parading in uniform in Summit Hill on August 2, 1851. Subsequent diary entries indicate that this marching was a common occurrence.

In early September 1851 the "Guards" underwent an inspection at Summit Hill. According to the newspaper report, this military corps, although very skilled at drill, was "completely new" and only needed "arms and accoutrements" to be complete.[219]

Problems with Coal Dirt

DURING THE YEAR 1858 the LC&N faced additional challenges.

Over the many decades since coal mining had commenced in the Panther Valley, heaps of coal dirt and breaker waste had accumulated, creating towering banks, which, as expected, drained into the Panther Creek, which carried these fines into the Little Schuylkill River at Tamaqua, which then carried them into the Schuylkill River itself.

Waste piles from anthracite coal breakers tower over the Panther Creek. Many of these waste piles, called "culm" banks, burned with a reddish hue and emitted sulphureous fumes. The coal breakers and the culm banks fascinated those tourists who spent the extra money for a tour around the Panther Valley. Bob Gormley

In the Fall of 1858, the Schuylkill Navigation Company finally communicated concerns to the LC&N, that the dirt from

> certain of the mines of this Company, is so disposed of as to be washed into and injure their navigation, it was on motion resolved, that the Superintendent & Engineer be directed to have the evil complained of, arrested as speedily and economically as practicable.[220]

To alleviate the problem, the LC&N by the end of 1858 the LC&N constructed

> a dam across the lower part of Panther Creek Valley, so as to form a reservoir to arrest the dirt; this reservoir covering a surface of more than seven acres, will, it is believed, hold all the dirt that will be brought down for several years.[221]

Panther Valley Summary Timeline: 1859

➤ February 1859: A fire was accidentally set in Slope No. 1.
➤ March 1859: LC&N executed the following 3-year mining contracts:
  • Fellows and Van Horn for Tunnel No. 7.
  • Robert A. Abbott and Hugh S. Davis for Tunnel No. 8.
  • James McLean for Tunnels No. 5 and No. 6.
➤ Slope No. 4 was driven down 50 yards, and support equipment installed.
➤ Late 1859: LC&N began the elimination of the Sharp Mountain inclined plane.
➤ December 23, 1859: Death of Edwin A. Douglas.

Sharp Mountain Plane Abandoned

ALTHOUGH THE SHARP MOUNTAIN inclined plane was only in use 9 years, in 1859 the LC&N abandoned that incline.[222]

This change eventually involved not only eliminating the Sharp Mountain inclined plane, but also abandoning the Springvale Switch-Backs. Since the Sharp Mountain plane handled loaded cars from Slope No. 2, this change also involved re-routing loaded coal cars from Slope No. 2 to the foot of inclined plane No. 1, requiring increasing the power of that incline, since it would have to handle loaded car traffic from Springvale Tunnel, Slope No. 2 and Tunnel No. 2, as well as Tunnels No. 3 and 4. This power increase was accomplished by installing larger engines and adding five new steam boilers to those already in operation. A new descending track was laid, closely conformed to the grade of the mountainside, allowing the famous Springvale switches to be eliminated.[223]

This work was begun in 1859 and completed in 1860.

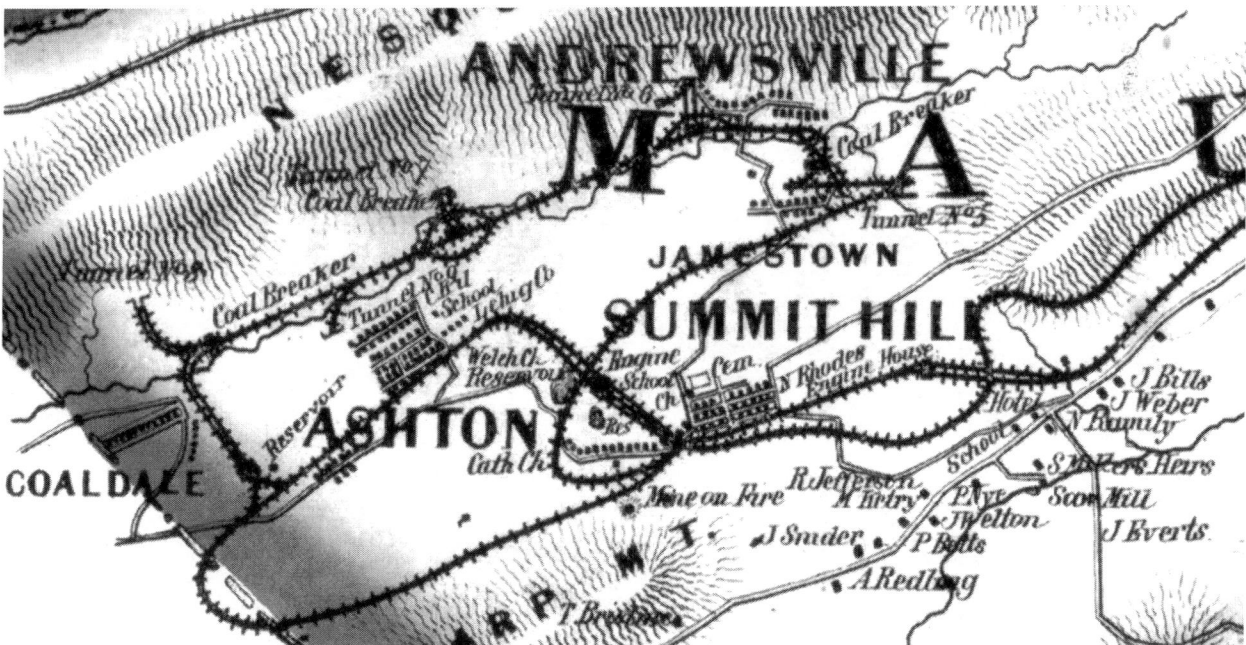

This section of the 1860 *Map of Carbon and Monroe Counties* shows that both the Springvale switch-Backs and the Sharp Mountain Plane had been eliminated by that date, while the Jamestown switch-backs remained in use.

More Slopes

DURING 1859 the LC&N signed a contract to drive Slope No. 4 in the eastern end of the Panther Valley near the summit above Tunnel No. 5. During the year the slope was driven down almost 50 yards, and the engines and boilers and hoisting apparatus were installed.[224]

That year the LC&N also began sinking Slope No. 8 within Tunnel No. 8.[225]

To Contractors.

Office Lehigh Coal & Nav. Co.,
Mauch Chunk, Nov. 10, 1859.
PROPOSALS will be received at this office until the 28th inst., for sinking a slope at Tunnel No. 8 of the Lehigh Company's Mines. For specifications and further information, apply to Nathan Patterson or Josiah McMurtrie, Summit Hill, or the undersigned at this place.
nov12-3t   E. A. DOUGLAS,
                         Sup't & Eng'r.

Carbon Democrat 12 Nov 1859, DML

The Burning Mine

IN FEBRUARY 1859 A FIRE was accidentally ignited in the underground workings of Slope No. 1, located near the Summit Mines. The Company's Engineer reported that

> Measures will shortly be taken to prevent the fire from extending to the working mines. It can doubtless be kept under control, and will be ultimately extinguished.[226]

These expectations turned out to be highly optimistic. Although the fire threatened the vast mineral wealth of the LC&N, it continued to spread and within several decades the "Burning Mines" of Summit Hill would prove to be a boon to the tourist economy of Summit Hill. Eventually excursions were run on the Switchback Railroad, and Summit Hill children served as tour guides for those wishing to view the "attraction."

BURNING MINE SHOWING SURFACE EFFECT
SUMMIT HILL, PA.

The Summit Hill Burning Mines from a twentieth century picture postcard. After the Panther Valley portion of the Switchback was removed from service, tourists needed new sites to visit. The Summit Hill Ice Cave and Burning Mines provided this diversion.

Leisenring Takes Charge

ON DECEMBER 23, 1859, the Company's longtime Superintendent and Engineer, Edwin A. Douglas, suddenly died. The Board of Managers unanimously voiced their

> sorrow, of the decease of one, so long in the service of the Company, that his name had become identified with the history of their improvements in the Lehigh Region, and to whose intelligence, practical ability, professional skill and untiring energy, the Company are largely indebted for their triumph over obstacles, at one time, deemed almost insuperable; and for the present excellent condition of their works.[227]

On February 8, 1860 the Board appointed John Leisenring, Jr. one-time Panther Creek Valley contractor, as the new Superintendent and Engineer. Although the *Mauch Chunk Coal Gazette* reported that the position of Chief Engineer was filled by Daniel Bertsch, Jr., in reality, the LC&N

John Leisenring in the 1880s, Matthews and Hungerford, History of Carbon and Lehigh Counties

tapped Bertsch to be Leisenring's Principal Assistant Engineer. The company would not regret either of these choices.[228] Leisenring was hired at an annual salary of $3,000 per year plus dwelling and fuel, a fantastic deal for the LC&N, since Douglas had been hired 25 years earlier at a salary of $3500. Since Leisenring was involved in many other endeavors, the Board stipulated that

"it being the express understanding that the said John Leisenring will give his whole time and energy exclusively to the business of the Company." [229]

Leisenring entered upon his duties with alacrity, and on March 6 submitted a report outlining proposed solutions to some of the Company's most pressing problems. Leisenring would also begin moving forward with preparations for replacing the Valley's gravity railroads with a locomotive railroad.[230] In his report to the LC&N Board of Managers Leisenring submitted a plan to deal with the mine fire in the underground

Parkhurst was John Leisenring's residence in Mauch Chunk until his death in 1884. Built by Josiah White in the 1830s, it became the residence of successive LC&N superintendents. Leisenring eventually bought the building outright from the LC&N. Clarence Hendricks

85

workings of Slope No. 1. This plan included making open cuts above ground to retard the progress of the fire as well as raising the water level in the mines to a height sufficient to smother the flames. Neither solution would prove effective at spreading the underground conflagration.[231]

Panther Valley Summary Timeline: 1860

➢ February 8, 1860: John Leisenring, Jr. hired to replace Edwin Douglas.

➢ LC&N eliminated Sharp Mountain Inclined Plane No. 3 and replaced the Springvale Switch-Backs with a long sweeping curve.

➢ The entire length of the "Old Switch-Back" the Valley's First Return Backtrack, extending from the Summit past the head of Plane No. 2 to the foot of Plane No. 1 was relaid with T-rails weighing 32 lbs. to the yard.

➢ Work was started on a new railroad from Slope No. 4 to the foot of Panther Creek Plane No. 1.

➢ The power of hoisting at Panther Creek Plane No. 1 increased by replacing the engines with those of more power and adding 5 additional boilers.

Dry Hollow

IN SPITE OF CONTINUING OVERPRODUCTION within the coal industry, the LC&N continued its own expansion plans, intending to sink Slope No. 6 on the mountainside above Tunnel No. 2 at a location known as "Dry Hollow. In the Fall of 1860, Leisenring was directed to contract for 68 tons of railroad iron to lay a line from this slope to intersect the Panther Creek Railroad near the Springvale Tunnel. Grading of this railroad began shortly thereafter, however, it was never completed. Instead of a slope at Dry Hollow, Tunnel No. 11 would later be driven further west to attack the same veins.[232]

The Failure of Foster's Tunnel

TUNNEL NO 2 AND ITS EXCLUSIVE RAILROADS and inclined planes can probably be considered one of the biggest engineering failures in the Panther Valley. While the tunnel was originally opened in 1846, it did not produce any coal until 1857 when slightly more than 10,000 tons were produced. That figure declined to 7,600 tons the following year and in 1859 only 71 tons came out of that tunnel.

Beginning in 1858 valley contractor George Kline signed the first of several yearly leases of Tunnel No. 2.[233] Initially the tunnel struck some good coal, but it failed soon after, encountering only slatey, broken coal, leading Kline to contact the LC&N managers

representing his pecuniary difficulties and soliciting relief from the Company.[234]

Over the years 1859 to 1873 the LC&N spent insignificant sums of money driving new gangways in Tunnel No. 2 in a largely unsuccessful attempt to find marketable coal. Sometime between 1873 and 1882, when the tunnel reached marketable coal, a railroad would be constructed from Tunnel No. 2 to Colliery 11 near Tamaqua.

Railroad Development in
the Panther Valley ca 1860

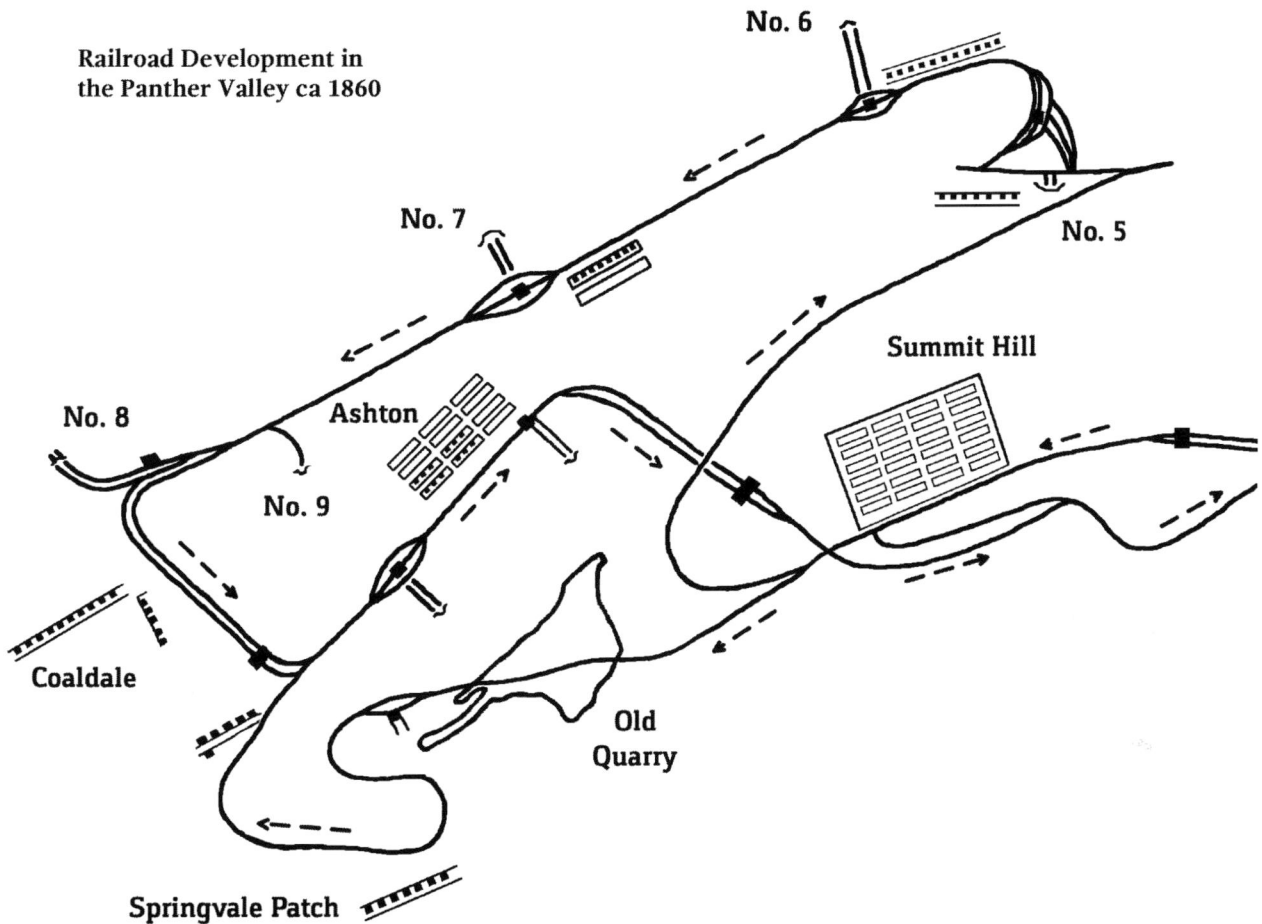

No. 6

No. 7

No. 5

No. 8

Ashton

Summit Hill

No. 9

Coaldale

Old
Quarry

Springvale Patch

Railroad Development in the Panther Valley circa 1860. By 1860 the Foster's Tunnel inclined plane and backtrack had been removed, along with the Sharp Mountain inclined plane. The Summit Hill breaker had also been removed. The Springvale return track into the Valley was completely redesigned, eliminating the famous switch-backs that gave the railroad its popular name. Map adapted by the author from various sources

Panther Valley Summary Timeline: 1861

➤ April 12, 1861: Start of the United States Civil War.
➤ April 12, 1861: State of Pennsylvania chartered the Nesquehoning Valley Railroad (hereafter NVRR).
➤ May 14, 1861: Act for constructing NVRR became law.
➤ LC&N began digging an "open deep cut" between Slopes 1 and 2, to stop the mine fire.
➤ Completed railroad from Slope No. 4 to the foot of Panther Creek Plane No. 1.
➤ LC&N began driving Tunnel No. 10.

Limited Demand for Coal, Limited Work Opportunities

FOLLOWING THE ECONOMIC DOWNTURN that began in 1857, the anthracite industry continued to suffer from overproduction. That problem would not be remedied until the Civil War drastically increased the demand for coal.

In their report to the stockholders for the performance of the Company during 1861, the LC&N observed:

> In consequence of the limited demand for coal during the greater part of the season of 1861, the Company's Panther Creek mines were worked for only about four days in the week and resulted in a large falling off from the usual yearly quantity of coal mined and shipped to market.[235]

The LC&N continued to respond to the depression in the coal trade by opening new mines to gain control of more of the anthracite market. This would include driving new tunnels within its usual operating lands, and seeking entry into coal regions outside the Valley. This would require a new railroad.

A War to Change Everything

ON APRIL 12, 1861, at 4:30 am the Confederate State of South Carolina began the bombardment of Fort Sumter, an act that would have serious repercussion for the United States, for the Lehigh Coal and Navigation Company and the Panther Creek Valley. The LC&N would meet these challenges, and others, and survive well into the next century.

Eli Conner's Tunnel

IN APTIL OF 1861 the LC&N Board of Managers accepted a proposal from Eli Taylor Conner to drive Tunnel No. 10 on the north side of the Panther Creek Valley west of Tunnel No. 8. The contract specified that the tunnel was to be about 1200 feet long, and was to be driven night and day, Sundays excepted, such that the work would be completed before February 1, 1863. Conner would not live to see the work completed.[236]

Biographical Digression: Eli Taylor Conner (1832-1862)

BORN IN LUZERNE COUNTY in 1832, Eli Conner moved to Mauch Chunk with his parents in 1833. After his education, which included a military

Eli T. Conner. J.D. Laciar, *Patriotism of Carbon County*, Mauch Chunk, 1867, 60

academy, Conner was hired as a civil engineer during the construction of Asa Packer's Lehigh Valley Railroad. In June of 1855 Conner married Asa Lansford Foster's daughter Mary Chapman. Conner and wife left Mauch Chunk and headed south a month later, to Conner's next job on the Cape Fear River canal system near Wilmington, North Carolina.

The Conners did not appreciate the heat and humidity of the south, and returned north in the summer of 1856, when upon the recommendation of Edwin Douglas, LC&N Managers offered Eli

Conner the position of Superintendent of the Lehigh and Susquehanna Railroad at a salary of $900 per year. Conner turned down the offer, however, and returned to a position on the LVRR, where he surveyed the Penn Haven and White Haven Railroad during the winter of 1859-1860.

Conner also served his country's military, serving in both the Carbon Guards, where he was 1st Lieutenant and as Captain of the Cleaver Artillerists.[237]

In early 1861 the LC&N awarded Conner the contract to drive Tunnel No. 10 in the Panther Valley; the start of the US Civil War followed a few days later. Within twenty-four hours of President Lincoln's first call for troops, Conner recruited three full companies. He served as captain of the Pennsylvania Volunteers from April 22 to July 22, 1861.

It is not known who took over Conner's tunnel No. 10 mining contract, but on October 1st of 1861 Conner was commissioned as Major of the 81st Regiment, Pennsylvania Volunteers, Company G, and the following year was promoted to Lieutenant Colonel. While fighting in the war both his wife and son died of Tuberculosis. In July of 1862 Conner himself was killed in the battle at Malvern Hill, Virginia. In 1865 Asa Lansford Foster and his son Thomas Lansford Foster journeyed to Virginia to recover the body of Conner. They left on May 22 and returned to Mauch Chunk on June 1. On June 7 Eli Conner was re-interred in the Upper Mauch Chunk cemetery.[238]

Eli Taylor Conner's monument in the cemetery in the heights section of Jim Thorpe is shared, not only with his wife and son, but also with Asa Lansford Foster and Isaac Abel Chapman.

The Nesquehoning Valley Railroad

IN 1861 A SEVERE DROP in demand for anthracite coal, leading to a production decline at LC&N mines of almost 100,000 tons for the year, caused complaint from the LC&N managers, who saw expansion of coal production as a necessary response. In addition to plans to expand coal production at Room Run and within the Panther Valley, the LC&N Managers forecast the need to expand into new geographical regions, including the Mahanoy region. To do this a new railroad would be required, passing through the Nesquehoning Valley

> by the construction of which, with extraordinary advantages of grade and distance, one of the finest coal fields in the State will be brought into direct and close connexion with the Company's canal near Mauch Chunk, and a large and valuable addition made to the Company's business.[239]

In September of 1861 Mauch Chunk newspapers reported that surveying the route for the Nesquehoning Valley Railroad (hereinafter NVRR) had been completed. By then, plans to use this railroad to eliminate the gravity railroads had been leaked to the press.

> Among other things, the company will drive a tunnel through the mountain from Panther Creek Valley into the Nesquehoning, at Breaker No. 7, which will make an outlet from Panther Creek to the Lehigh at M. Chunk . . . The tunnel will be about 4000 feet long, of which about one-third is already made, but requires enlargement.[240]

This photo shows the coal breaker for Panther Valley Tunnel No. 7, constructed in 1850 and dismantled circa 1868, after the LC&N decided to use the tunnel as a locomotive route through the Locust (Nesquehoning) Mountain. Bob Gormley

Originally planned as a means for the LC&N to extend its reach into the Mahanoy coal region, there can be little doubt that the Company envisioned it as a more efficient method of getting coal out of the Panther Creek Valley, and from Room Run.   If indeed there had been no thought of tying the NVRR into a full-scale railroad project, the Great Flood of June 1862 would change all that.

Panther Valley Summary Timeline: 1862

- ➤ June 3: Great Flood of the Lehigh River.
- ➤ James McLean contracted to work Tunnel No. 5 for 2 years.
- ➤ Wm Sharpe and AJ Wintersteen contracted to work Tunnel No. 8 and Slope No. 5 for 3 years.
- ➤ LC&N authorized construction of ten blocks of miner's houses at Slope No. 4, Tunnel No. 5, at an estimated cost of $750 each.
- ➤ LC&N rebuilt Inclined Plane No. 1 Plane House with heavy stone masonry walls and slate roofing.
- ➤ LC&N completed the coal breaker at Slope No. 4.
- ➤ LC&N continued driving Tunnel No. 10.
- ➤ At the Summit continued the deep excavation at Slope No. 2 to cut off the burning mine fire.

The flood of the Lehigh River at Mauch Chunk on October 4, 1869, not as severe as that of 1862, from which no photos appear to have survived. From stereoviews by Mauch Chunk photographer Joseph Brown

The Great Flood of 1862

NOT ONLY DID THE WAR BETWEEN THE STATES severely impact LC&N operations, nature herself again intervened in Company affairs.

Although the Lehigh Navigation had experienced several floods and freshets since the ice freshet of 1841, none was so terrible as the one that came in June of 1862, while the Company and nation were engaged in dealing with challenges of the Civil War.

Heavy rains began on the afternoon of June 3. The torrent fell without cease for over thirty hours without the LC&N managers worrying about the navigation. Following each of the previous floods, they had spent more money than was necessary to identify and strengthen weak points, expecting that the navigation would survive future floods. They viewed the added cost as an investment.

Growth and settlement and a booming lumber business in the upper section of the Lehigh Valley brought more dams feeding sawmills along the tributary streams draining into the Lehigh. It is likely that clear cutting of forests in the upper section was a contributing factor for the flood.

Even with the torrential rains, dams on the Lehigh Navigation stood fast, and the Lehigh rose higher than it had ever risen in its history. However, just as the river attained its maximum volume, lumber booms near the head of the navigation broke, sending between 200,000 and 300,000 cut logs down the river with incredible force. These logs were responsible for the terrible damage and loss of life sustained throughout the valley.

These logs acted as battering rams, pummeling the guard banks so that they gave way, pulling the wooden dams with them. As each dam succumbed another swell of water was added to the torrent, so that the valley was hammered by a sequence of waves, each one adding momentum to the wooden battering rams.

The water level at Mauch Chunk reached a maximum of 27 feet above normal low water, 10 feet higher than during the flood of 1841. John Leisenring later estimated that somewhere between 100 and 200 persons lost their lives.

This flood brought John Leisenring his biggest challenge as LC&N Superintendent and Engineer. He ordered the complete suspension of all operations, which remained in effect until the re-opening of the Lehigh Canal in October.[241]

In addition to destroying the Lehigh Navigation, the heavy rains completely flooded out several of the Panther Valley mines, including Slope No. 3, which became so flooded that the mine could not be re-opened for the remainder of 1862.

Despite material and labor shortages the LC&N was able to resume navigation in early October. However, the cost of repairing the Upper Division of the Navigation convinced the LC&N to replace that part of the navigation with a locomotive railroad, one that would eventually stretch from Wilkes-Barre in the north to Easton in the South, and one that would compete with Asa Packer's Lehigh Valley Railroad.

Panther Valley Summary Timeline: 1863

➢ LC&N deals with "unrest" at its mines.
➢ LC&N continued working Tunnel No. 10.
➢ Leisenring officially proposed constructing a railroad through Tunnel No. 7 to eliminate the gravity railroads within the valley.
➢ Fall of 1863: Work began on the Coalport Shipping Docks, 1 mile north of Mauch Chunk.

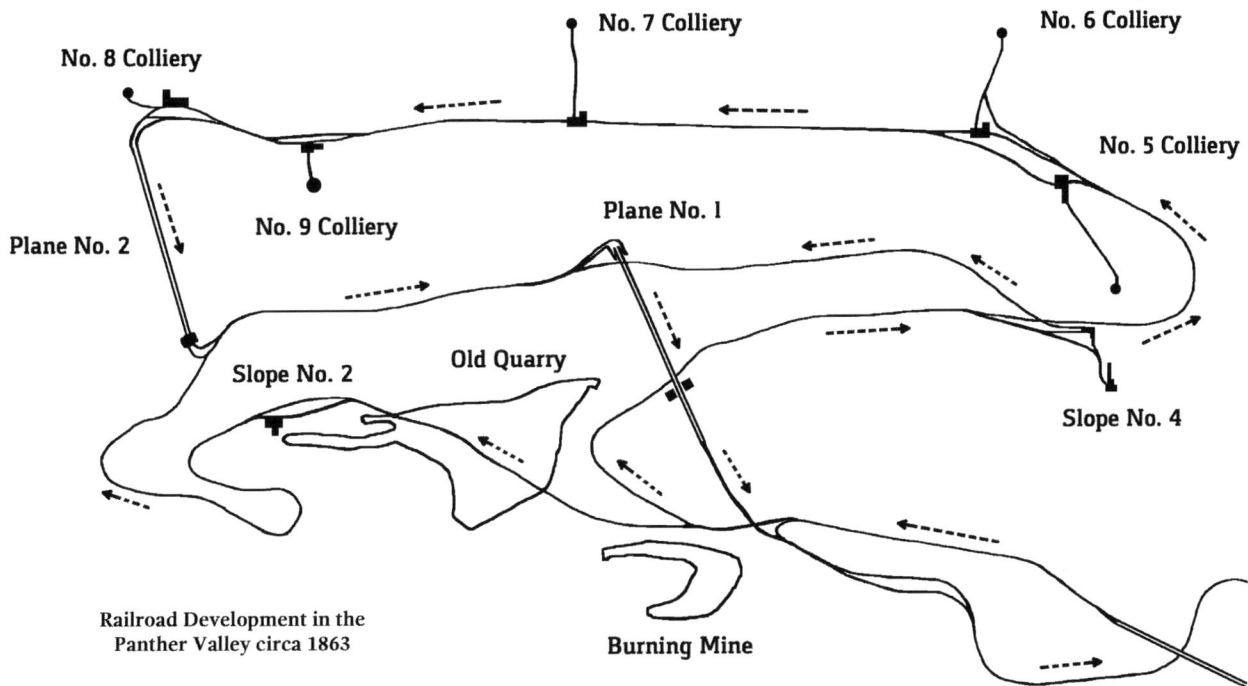

Panther Valley Railroad Development circa 1863. During 1859 the LC&N began driving Slope No. 4 down the east end of the Valley. In 1860 the company started work on a railroad from this slope to the foot of Panther Creek Plane No. 1 and completed it in 1861. The "switch-backs" at No. 5, Jamestown were eliminated circa 1862. Developed by the author from various maps and other sources

Civil War Problems

THE CIVIL WAR INTRODUCED other problems for the LC&N, draining off laborers to supply the Union's war machine. As a result, LC&N Managers found it the necessary to raise prices paid to the coal contractors in amounts ranging from 10 to 13 cents per ton.[242] Despite this action, as early as January of 1863 "disorder" spread throughout the coal region. LC&N Superintendent and Engineer John Leisenring reported

> that the widely spread disorder, and the demand for increased wages of the miners, prevailing in the Coal regions generally, had reached such a crisis that it was imperatively necessary for the Company to make a further advance on the contract prices, to enable the contractors to keep their hands at work in the mines.[243]

The Board agreed and authorized Leisenring to "make the best arrangement he can with the contractors to meet the present emergency." [244]

The War inflation had other impacts on the LC&N's ability to continue operations. At a meeting with the Board Leisenring reported that the houses previously authorized to be constructed at

> Slope No. 4 Tunnel No. 5, at an estimated cost of $750 per block of two houses each not having yet been erected, could not now be put up for less than $925 per block.

As before Leisenring was directed to proceed with the work.[245]

At a stockholder's meeting in May of 1864 Leisenring summarized the challenges the Company faced during 1863:

The Company's mines were not, owing to the great demand for miners and mine laborers, worked with the usual regularity of former years. The high rates of wages obtained throughout the region for this class of labor, tended to unsettle the men, and frequent strikes for higher wages, &c., was the result of the extraordinary demand for mine operatives, to which the Company's mines were in some measure subjected, though not to so great an extent as in some other portions of the coal region.[246]

Tunnel No. 10

IN 1863 THE ISSUE OF TUNNEL No. 10 had also been resurrected. In April Leisenring suggested that the price for driving the mine should be increased to $8.50 per lineal yard. The Board agreed with Leisenring's recommendation, and a contract was signed with Thomas Craig to grade a 1 ¾ mile railroad from the tunnel to the foot of Panther Creek Plane No. 2. The railroad required 138 tons of 50 lb. T rail and was expected to cost $14,000. Twelve blocks of double houses were built near the tunnel, at an expected cost of $660 per block.[247]

The Burning Mine

THE LC&N CONTINUED EFFORTS to "check the progress" of the burning mine fire. In September of 1863 a correspondent to Mauch Chunk's *Carbon Democrat*, after touring the Panther Valley operations, observed progress to date:

> In my ramblings my guide led me to what is called the "Open Cut." This is one of the most extensive undertakings imaginable. It is a very large trough cut north and south across the mountain, which runs east and West, clearing away rock and coal, to check the progress of the burning coal vein.[248]

Leisenring's Bold Proposal for the Future

IN NOVEMBER 1863 THE LC&N Board of Managers read a extraordinary letter from John Leisenring

A view of the burning mines at Summit Hill.
Lee Mantz

advocating a change in the present mode of transporting coal from the mines in the Panther Valley to Mauch Chunk by submitting locomotive power through a tunnel under the mountain on the north side of the basin and down the proposed Nesquehoning Valley Rail Road in lieu of the system now in use of inclined planes and gravity roads.[249]

Leisenring proposed abandoning coal extraction in tunnel No. 7 and extending it clear through the mountain, at an estimated cost of $177,500. Since the mine was in the mountain between Tunnels No. 6 and 8, the veins could still be exploited from gangways extended from both these tunnels. The Board immediately approved Leisenring's plan and instructed him to place the work under contract.[250]

Things would not go according to plan.

Although Leisenring had been instructed to extend Tunnel No. 7 through to the Panther Valley as early as November of 1863, nothing was done at that time, due to the labor shortage from the ongoing Civil War.[251]

Although Leisenring initially took credit for this idea, he later learned and admitted, in a letter to Josiah White's son-in-law Richard Richardson, that White himself had conceived the plan.[252]

The Coalport Shipping Docks

WHILE THE WORK OF TUNNELING through the Nesquehoning Mountain into the Panther Valley would be delayed, the Company moved briskly forward with plans for their new railroad down the Lehigh, including coal pockets north of Mauch Chunk.

During the fall of 1863 construction was already underway on the Coalport Pockets. While designed to transfer coal from the Wyoming Valley to canal boats, these pockets would eventually replace the Mauch Chunk Switchback Railroad coal schutes, and transship coal from the Panther Valley.

Coalmine tunnel No. 7 in the Panther Valley while it was still being worked. In January 1846 the LC&N awarded the contract to drive this tunnel to James Broderick and his partner, a man named Ryan. In 1869 the LC&N began extending this tunnel through the mountainside to connect the mines of the Panther Valley with the Nesquehoning Valley Railroad, a branch of the L&S RR. On February 2, 1872, the first train from the Panther Valley passed through the new tunnel, thus numbering the days of the Switchback as a coal hauler. George Harvan

Panther Valley Summary Timeline: 1864

On August 1, 1864, a new railroad, designed for locomotives, leading from Tunnel No. 10 to the foot of Panther Creek Plane No. 2 was completed. In addition, the coal breaker for the tunnel, along with "associated fixtures" was put into service, allowing coal to be produced for the remainder of the season.

In 1864 new wire ropes were installed on both Panther Creek planes, and worn-out boilers for Plane No. 2 engine house were replaced with new ones. The decayed crossties on the track from the head of Plane No. 2 to the foot of plane No. 1 were also replaced.

The breaker for Panther Valley Tunnel No. 10. This is probably a photo of the second breaker. The first breaker was completed in 1865 and abandoned in 1881. Bob Gormley

Panther Valley Summary Timeline: 1865

➢ January 1 to March 10, 1865: Strike of valley miners.

➢ April 9, 1865: End of the War Between the States.

➢ In 1865 the LC&N introduced a locomotive into the valley.

➢ Summer 1865:. The LC&N lowered miners wages from $1.50 to 75 cents per car.

➢ December 1865: Superintendent and Engineer John Leisenring proposed eliminating contracting in the valley, by hiring miners and managers directly.

Continuing Labor Unrest in the Valley

AS THE WAR BETWEEN THE STATES CONTINUED, so did labor unrest. In the Southern Anthracite region, Schuylkill County mines saw the greatest trouble, but Carbon County was not immune. From January 1 to March 10, 1865, LC&N miners and laborers turned out, more than likely for higher wages. The strike was unsuccessful, and

> the men went to work again on the Company's terms; and no further difficulty occurred with them during the remainder of the year. But for this strike, the yield of the mines would have been considerably in excess of that of the preceding year.[253]

Possibly due to the labor issues, in 1865, Leisenring recommended the elimination of contract letting in the Valley.

> Instead of contracting with a single individual or firm for the mining and preparation of the coal, at prices made to vary with the cost of labor and materials, it is proposed that the miners and laborers shall be employed directly by the Company, under the supervision of an inside foreman, and an outside foreman, the men to be paid however, as far as practicable, according to the quantity of coal mined.[254]

In the Company's Annual Report, published several months later, the Managers related the reasons for this major change in policy:

> It has been found impossible for several years past, amidst the great fluctuations in the prices of labor and of all commodities, to hold the contractors for a term of years to a fixed price for mining and preparing coal. This looseness has removed much of the inducement that operated in former times to stimulate them to a close and economical management of their business, and has left us, it is thought, without sufficient compensation, to the disadvantage of having the mining conducted by parties much less interested than the Company are in having the mines worked clean, and with the least possible waste of coal. The contracts for working several of the mines having expired with the close of last year, these mines have been placed in charge of the mining engineer, with instructions to have the coal mined and prepared under his own directions, without the intervention of a contractor at each colliery.[255]

The LC&N would reconsider, somewhat, their plans just a few years later. On January 1, 1868, Leisenring, after reporting the condition of the company's property, noted the following:

> After careful consideration, I have come to the conclusion that it would be good policy for the Company to lease its Panther Creek and Room Run Mines provided that arrangements can be made with responsible parties on favorable terms, and confine its operations to a transportation business. The Company would thus be relieved from a very troublesome branch of its business, which requires the use of a large amount of capital.[256]

However, Leisenring's recommendation was not for a return to the practice of contracting to individuals, but to lease the entire mining operation to a single business entity. This would happen within the next decade.

End of the Civil War

THE GOOD NEWS IN 1865, was the end of the war between the states, following the surrender of the Confederacy at Appomattox on April 9, 1865. As with most events, there was a negative impact as well. The demand for coal collapsed as the war machine of the Industrial North scaled back.

This photo of the early locomotive "Catawissa" circa 1860, was most likely the type of locomotive integrated into Panther Valley operations in 1865. From a stereopticon slide

Locomotives in the Valley

AN IMPORTANT CHANGE for the Panther Valley, indeed for all the LC&N's mining operations, was the introduction of a locomotive into the Valley.

According to a story in the *History of St. Mary's Church of Coaldale, Pa.*, in 1866 the LC&N introduced the first locomotive to Panther Valley mining. However, LC&N records, peg this to 1865.

> Coal from Tunnel No. 10, which was heretofore hauled to the foot of Plane No. 2 . . . with mule teams, is now transported by steam power, a third rail having been introduced last spring, so that a locomotive engine of 4 feet 8 1/2 inches gauge could be used.[257]

This locomotive

> was shipped from Philadelphia by way of the Philadelphia and Reading Railroad, and from Tamaqua made its way on rails, temporarily laid in sections. When the locomotive had traversed a given length mules dragged the section ahead again, and the operation was repeated until Coaldale was reached. Here it was greeted by what was considered an immense crowd of people who stood about in open-mouthed wonder.[258]

Locomotives were not quite new to LC&N mines.   Two years earlier, the contractors at Nesquehoning's Room Run mines had replaced mule power on the Room Run Railroad with a locomotive, hauled from Tamaqua, presumably using the same method as the locomotive for Tunnel No. 10.[259]

These locomotives were so successful at eliminating mule power, that they were soon introduced inside the mines, as well. In May of 1868 Mauch Chunk newspapers reported:

> An Engine for Mines. On Thursday we saw a locomotive engine at this place, which is intended to be used in the Lehigh Coal and Navigation Co.'s mines . . . The engine is 12 feet long, 6 feet high, and has a capacity of about 7 horsepower. . . It is to perform the work of 30 mules, and if it proves a success, will be a valuable addition to the mining facilities. On Thursday afternoon it was taken by wagon to the mines, and probably by this time is performing its underground work.[260]

Mauch Chunk newspapers, however, reported that the engine proved to be a "Complete Failure."

> The mining engine intended to be run in the mines of the Lehigh Coal and Nav. Company, at Summit Hill, an account of which we gave a few weeks since, has proven itself a complete failure. It was brought back to Mauch Chunk on Wednesday and re-shipped to the builders at Philadelphia.[261]

After modifications, the engine was returned in August.

> The Mining Engine. The diminutive engine of which we spoke a few weeks ago, as being a failure, has been remodeled to some extent, and again put to work in the mines. It works well now and will accomplish the work for which it is designed.[262]

In January of 1869 the LC&N's mining engineer Thomas Phillips reported the introduction of another mine engine:

> It will take the place of thirteen mules and three drivers, and will require twenty-five mine cars less for the same amount of coal, relieving us from the expense of building the twenty-five additional cars.[263]

In early 1872 the LC&N introduced still another locomotive, this one constructed from Baldwin and Company, for ". . . drawing the cars to and from the Panther Creek Mines to the Tunnel." [264] By 1876, after the LC&N shops had been moved from Summit Hill into the Valley, the LC&N was constructing its own engines.[265]

Panther Valley Summary Timeline: 1866

➤ January 1, 1866: LC&N began new system of hiring its own miners and laborers, rather than contractors.

➤ April 1866: LC&N lowered miners wages from 75 cents to 50 cents per car.

➤ April – May 1866: Short-lived strike of the valley miners.

➤ May 1866: LC&N's Summit Hill machine shop set on fire.

The New System

ON JANUARY 1, 1866, DUE TO THE EXPIRATION of mining contracts at several Panther Valley mines, the LC&N began operating Slopes No. 3, 4 and 5, and Tunnel No. 9, using its own miners and laborers. Leisenring planned to implement this method at the Company's remaining collieries, as contracts expired.[266]

When reporting on the new method in his Engineer's Report to the Stockholders on January 1, 1866, Leisenring was optimistic:

> I have no doubt it will be a decided improvement on the old system.[267]

Within only a few years Leisenring would think otherwise.

Another Strike

AS THE POST CIVIL WAR price of coal began and continued a persistent decline, coal operators saw no choice but to reduce wages. In April of 1866, following a "severe and dull winter" with little work for laborers, the LC&N lowered the price they would pay miners from 75 cents per car to 50 cents, a further reduction from $1.50 the miners had been receiving the summer of 1865.

Predictably, and perhaps the intended reaction, the miners struck.[268] The turnout was short-lived, with the men back at work by the end of May. However, negative feelings simmered, and within a week after the resumption of work, the LC&N's machine shop at Summit Hill was torched.[269] In addition, strikers at the Mauch Chunk shipping ports at Coalport and East Mauch Chunk prevented the loading of coal into canal boats. The President of the LC&N responded by recommending

> that the company engage a sufficient police force under the provisions of the act authorizing railroad companies to employ police force.[270]

In August of 1866 "persons unknown" blew up the safe in the LC&N's Summit Hill office but were frightened away before they could claim the $4000 in the safe. The LC&N offered a $1000 reward for "detection of the parties."[271]

Panther Valley Summary Timeline: 1868-1873

- 1868: R.P. Rothwell hired to provide a detailed map of LC&N mining property.
- January 11, 1869: Ground broke for NVRR near Lausanne Landing Tavern.
- May 4, 1869: Rothwell reports to the LC&N Board of Managers.
- Winter 1869-1870: NVRR completed from Catawissa RRR to L&SRR near the mouth of the Nesquehoning Creek.
- Spring 1870: NVRR "High Bridge" constructed.
- 1872: LC&N Shops and Offices moved to Ashton from Summit Hill. Construction of the "Big Office"
- 1872: Tourist travel on Panther Valley section of Switchback RR stopped.
- February 1, 1872: LC&N took possession of Lansford-Hauto Tunnel.
- November 1, 1872: Hauto Screen Building completed.
- December 1872: Panther Valley portion of the Switchback completely shutdown.

The LC&N Hires R.P. Rothwell

IN 1868, AS PART OF THE PANTHER VALLEY RAILROAD conversion plan, but also to obtain an accurate survey of the mining property in the Panther Valley, the LC&N hired Richard Pennefather Rothwell to survey the Company's Valley property and prepare a detailed report. This task was later extended to include Company property in the Wyoming Valley.[272]

At a meeting of the LC&N stockholders on May 4, 1869, Rothwell presented his report, and exhibited his map of the Panther Creek Valley, which included the planned connection to the NVRR.[273]

[Below] Adapted by the author from: Rothwell, Richard Pennefather. "Map of the Lehigh Coal & Navigation Co.'s Coal Property Near Mauch Chunk, Pa." Map. Philadelphia Pa.: P.S. Duval, Son & Co., 1869. *Norman B. Leventhal Map & Education Center*

Richard Pennefather Rothwell (1836-1901). Unknown Author. *The National Cyclopaedia of American Biography*, Volume X, 1900, 229

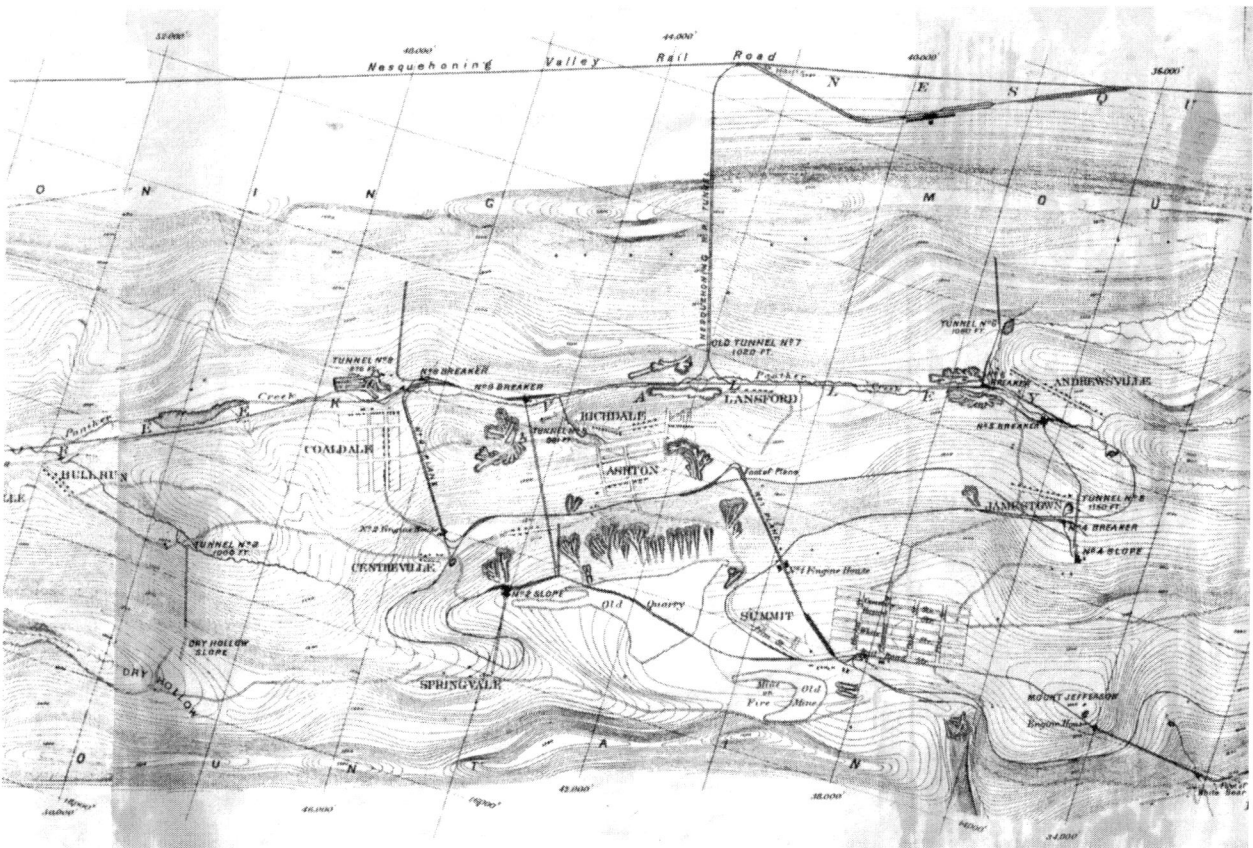

Nesquehoning Valley Railroad Continued

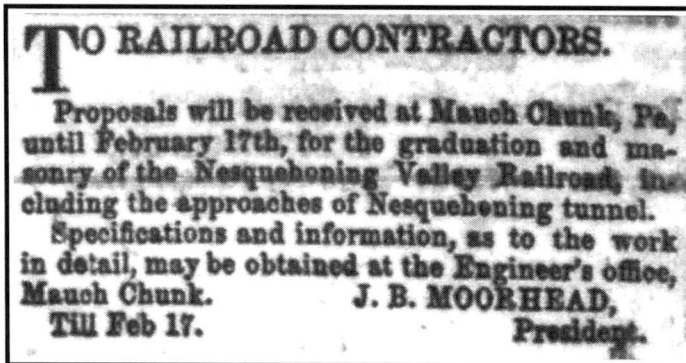

Carbon Democrat, 5 Feb 1869, DML

ALTHOUGH THE NVRR had been chartered as early as 1861, events interfered with company plans, so that by 1868 the LC&N still had not started construction of the railroad and the tunnel into the Panther Valley. Ground was finally broken for the NVRR near the Landing Tavern on the Lehigh River on January 11, 1869.[274]

Mauch Chunk newspapers reported

> This road is to run direct to all their coal operations and when completed will do away with the Summit Hill and Switch Back R. R. The Co. will gain largely by the building of the new road, but the public will regret to lose the famous Switch Back.[275]

During the Winter of 1869-1870 the NVRR was substantially completed from its connection with the Catawissa Railroad to the mouth of the Nesquehoning Creek, where it connected with the L&SRR. During Spring of 1870 the "High Bridge"

> over the Little Schuylkill on the Nesquehoning Valley Railroad, was tested by the successful and safe passage of an engine over it on Tuesday. Quite a crowd were in attendance to "celebrate" the event.[276]

On April 18, 1870 the LC&N took possession of the as-then-built NVRR, and on May 2 began running passenger and freight trains to the Catawissa. Work on the tunnel to the Panther Valley, however, remained incomplete.[277]

The LC&N vigorously pushed drilling of the tunnel. The two headings finally met on September 15, 1871, and five days later the last blast was fired. By January of 1872 railroad track extended halfway through the tunnel. At that time the breakers and coal mines in the Valley were temporarily shut down to allow laborers to widen the tracks in the valley for the use of locomotives.

The "High Bridge" over the Nesquehoning Valley Railroad following its completion in the early 1870s. Lippincott's *Magazine of Popular Literature and Science*, August 1872. "A Switchback Excursion," 134

On February 1, 1872, the LC&N took possession of the Lansford-Hauto Tunnel. The next day first locomotive train passed through the tunnel.[278]

Coal from the Panther Valley mines was soon regularly passing through the tunnel to the Coalport docks. In addition, the original gravity railroad, still in operation throughout 1872, was passing coal over the old gravity railroad. However, passenger travel to the public was discontinued, although special privileges were accorded to some local and visiting "dignitaries."

The first locomotive train through the Lansford – Hauto tunnel passed through on February 2, 1872. Estimates at the time predicted a savings of 20 cents per ton over transportation on the old gravity railroads. George Harvan

The Hauto Screen Building

AS PART OF THE OVERHAULED Panther Valley coal transportation system, the LC&N built a massive coal screening building for processing Panther Valley coal. This building was built on the north side of the Lansford Tunnel, in the Hauto Valley, on the Nesquehoning Valley Railroad. The screen building was completed and in operation by November 1 of 1872.[279]

The Hauto Screen building following completion of the Lansford-Hauto Tunnel and the Nesquehoning Valley Railroad. Bob Gormley

Final Panther Valley Timeline: 1873 and Beyond

➢ March 1873: Tracks on Panther Valley Inclined Plane No. 2 torn up.
➢ 1873: LC&N leased all its operations, including the Panther Valley Mines, to the Central Railroad of New Jersey and the Lehigh and Wilkes-Barre Coal Company.
➢ June 1874 the original gravity railroad still labelled the "Switch-Back" sold to the CRRNJ for $75,242.12.
➢ Spring 1876: Panther Valley railroad system extended to Summit Hill.
➢ 1877: Financial difficulties force CRRNJ & L&WBCC into receivership.
➢ January 1, 1878: LC&N regains control of its mining operations.

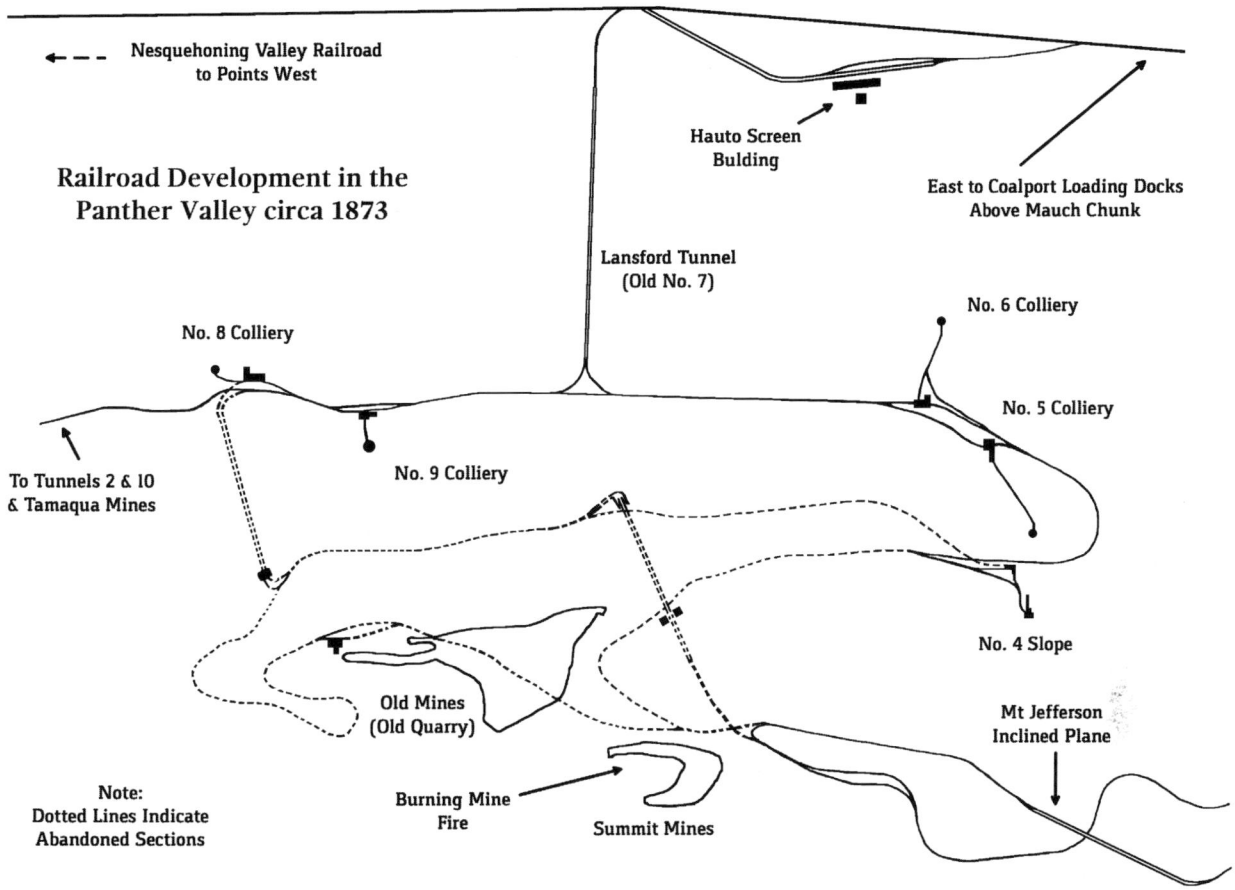

← - - - Nesquehoning Valley Railroad
to Points West

**Railroad Development in the
Panther Valley circa 1873**

Hauto Screen
Bulding

East to Coalport Loading Docks
Above Mauch Chunk

Lansford Tunnel
(Old No. 7)

No. 6 Colliery

No. 8 Colliery

No. 5 Colliery

To Tunnels 2 & 10
& Tamaqua Mines

No. 9 Colliery

No. 4 Slope

Old Mines
(Old Quarry)

Mt Jefferson
Inclined Plane

Note:
Dotted Lines Indicate
Abandoned Sections

Burning Mine
Fire

Summit Mines

Panther Valley Railroad Development circa 1873 after Tunnel No. 7 was extended clear through the Nesquehoning Mountain. This allowed railroads in the Panther Valley to connect with the NVRR, which was a branch of the LC&N's L&SRR. Map adapted by author from 1869 RP Rothwell Map and other sources

During 1872 the LC&N began moving its shops and offices from Summit Hill to Lansford. As part of this process, construction of a large office building, nicknamed the "Big Office," was begun in June 1872 and completed in 1873. The structure was destroyed by fire in 1975 and was razed soon after. Lansford *Valley Gazette*

The End of the Panther Valley Gravity Railroads

IN 1872 THE LC&N BEGAN the process of moving its shops and offices from Summit Hill into the valley proper. In June of 1872 construction was started on a massive office building near the Lansford side of the new tunnel, and completed the following year.[280]

The gravity railroad linking Summit Hill to the Panther Valley ceased operation at the end of the 1872 season. In March of 1873 the tracks on plane No. 2 were torn up.[281] The abandoned inclined planes proved useful as shortcut footpaths between the towns of Lansford and Summit Hill.[282] This was especially important as the Switch-Back had provided the only rail connection between the two towns. It wasn't until the spring of 1876 that Summit Hill was connected to Lansford's Panther Creek railroad, via a new track laid over the second return backtrack of the old Switchback. A connection was made to the Switchback railroad, permitting passengers from one railroad to transfer to the other.[283] The route of the second return backtrack was followed later by the Lansford - Summit Hill trolley.

The completion of the Nesquehoning Tunnel sealed the fate of gravity railroads in the Panther Valley and for the LC&N. John Leisenring would continue his association with the LC&N, but not as Superintendent and Engineer. He resigned this position in April 1868, but soon after came back to the LC&N as Chief Engineer, resigning that position later that year. By 1870 Leisenring was serving on the Executive Committee of the LC&N Board of Managers.[284]

TROLLEY ENTRANCE TO SUMMIT HILL, PA.

The shutdown of the Panther Valley gravity railroad removed the only rail connection between Summit Hill and Lansford. In Spring of 1876 this was remedied when a rail connection was laid over the abandoned backtrack from Summit Hill to the No. 5 area of the Panther Valley. The route was also used later for the Tamaqua-Lansford trolley. Ray Holland

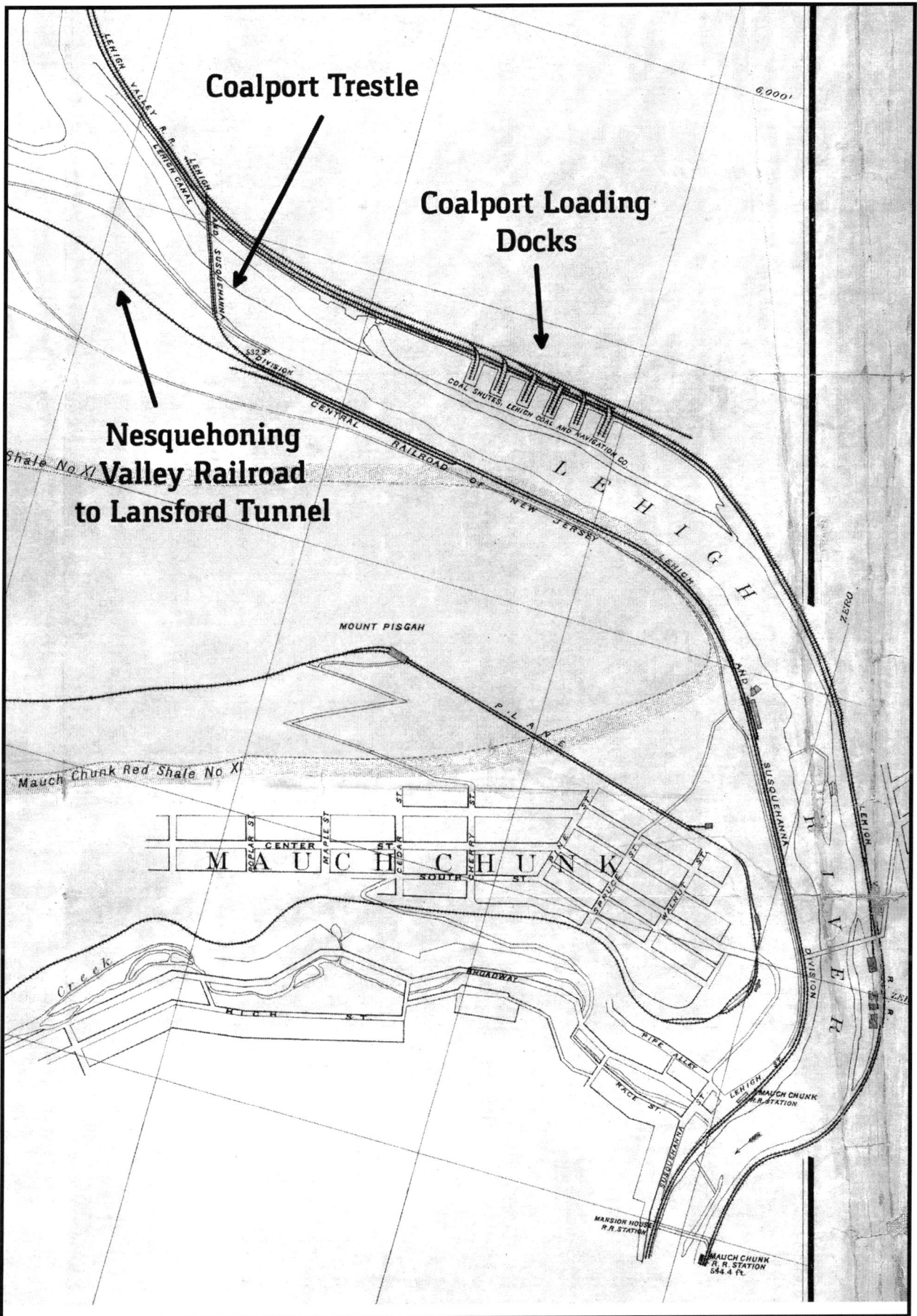

Coalport Trestle

Coalport Loading Docks

Nesquehoning Valley Railroad to Lansford Tunnel

[Previous Page] The LC&N's Lehigh and Susquehanna Railroad was extended from White Haven, through Mauch Chunk to Easton. Coal from the Lehigh Region was transshipped to canal boats at the "Coalport Pockets." Adapted by the author from an 1882 map, courtesy of Mauch Chunk Historical Society

[Above] "View from Mt. Pisgah-Looking North." The Coalport Loading docks from a stereopticon slide by MA Kleckner. The Village of Coalport, which was settled west of East Mauch Chunk to construct and support the shipping docks, is visible on the hillside above the shipping port.

[Top Next Page] An enlarged section of the previous map showing the Coalport docks. Lehigh Coal and Navigation Company coal from the Panther Valley and Nesquehoning mines shipped over the Lehigh and Susquehanna Railroad reached the Coalport docks via a trestle bridge across the Lehigh River at the Nesquehoning Junction. After December, 1872 they replaced the chutes at Mauch Chunk. The Coalport shipping docks remained in service until June 11, 1923, when they were replaced by a transfer shipping port at Laury's Station. Clarence Hendricks

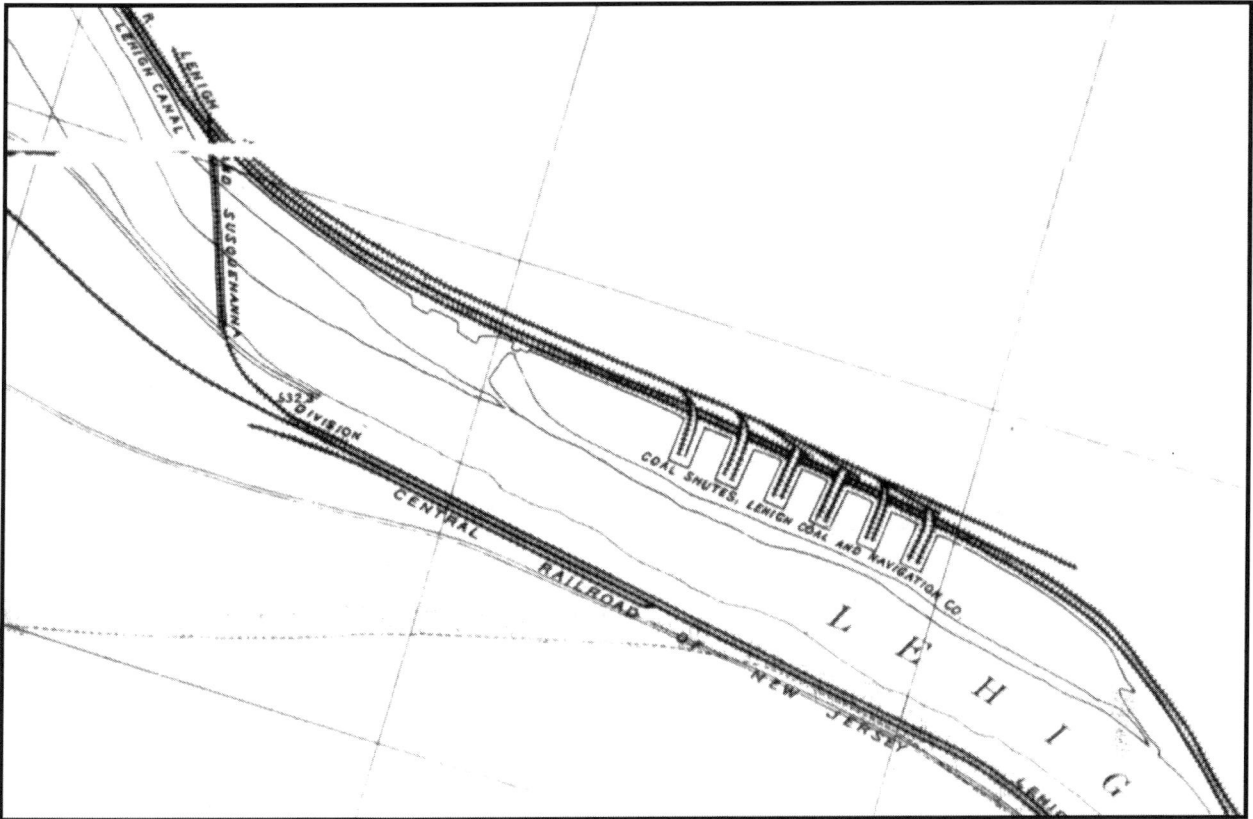

[Below] A closer view of the shipping basin at Coalport with a large canal boat moored at the left coal storage pocket. These shipping pockets were completed in mid-1865 and were connected to the Lehigh and Susquehanna Railroad.

The LC&N and the Central Railroad of New Jersey

IN 1873 THE LC&N WAS AGAIN faced with the specter of financial ruin, as demand for anthracite collapsed following the crash of the Jay Cooke banking house. That year, hoping to relieve itself and its Philadelphia officers of the burden of managing the extensive company operations, and manifest its age-old desire of being just a holding company, the LC&N leased all its coal property and transportation facilities to the Lehigh and Wilkes-Barre Coal Company and the Central Railroad of New Jersey.

When this happened, many of the local officers retained their jobs, working directly for the CRRNJ and the L&WBCC instead of the LC&N. But the LC&N leases, especially to the CRRNJ rarely if ever lived up to their promises. As a result, in 1877 the CRRNJ and L&WBCC were in receivership, with the LC&N regaining control of its mining properties on January 1, 1878.[285]

The Summit Hill-Mauch Chunk Gravity Road Continued

THE LEASE OF THE LC&N's properties included those in Nesquehoning and the Panther Creek Valley but did not include the portion of the original gravity railroad between Mauch Chunk and Summit Hill. In June 1874 this remaining property, still labelled the "Switch-Back" was sold to the Central Railroad for $75,242.12. This sale did not include the gravity railroad right of way between Mauch Chunk and Summit Hill.[286]

The Central Railroad owned the Switch-Back Railroad until October of 1929, leasing it to various individuals who operated it as a tourist attraction. The railroad remained a passenger carrier until October 1933 when the last pleasure car glided over the route. On September 2, 1937, the railroad, with all its fixtures, was auctioned off to a scrap dealer for $18,100.

Final Words

JOSIAH WHITE HAD ENVISIONED that expansion of mining into the Panther Creek Valley would ensure production of at least 500,000 tons of coal per year. This was barely achieved in 1872, the last year that coal was transported over the gravity railroad. That year Panther Valley and Summit Hill coal production inched up to 498,866 tons of coal.[287]

While most of the collieries in the Panther Valley shut down during the twentieth century, deep mining continued at Tunnel No. 9 until 1972, when shutdown of that tunnel finally ended deep mining in the Valley. However, strip mining in the Panther Valley, both to the east and to the west of the borough of Lansford, continues, as this history goes to press.

The history of Panther Creek Valley mining and railroad operations in the years after 1873 is grist for another mill.

Appendices

Appendix A
Tourists Ride the Rails Into Panther Creek Valley

EVEN BEFORE THE LC&N could spike down the last rail for the Summit Hill and Mauch Chunk gravity railroad, travelers passing through the region became obsessed by this latest American "internal improvement." They carried news of the railroad back to their home cities, where eager newspaper editors snatched up accounts of these visits for their papers. Completion and operation of the railroad brought even more fame. As early as June 2, 1827 the Schuylkill region's *Miner's Journal* referred to the gravity railroad as

> the 'Lion' of the day, and attracting an uncommon number of visitors from all parts of the country.[288]

The LC&N immediately began passenger service for traveling from Mauch Chunk to the mines, which were nine miles distant. Probably due to clamor from the visitors, soon even they were allowed on board, so long as the passenger travel did not interfere with the coal business.

Passenger Cars on the Switchback railroad such as this began descending into the Panther Creek Valley in the Spring of 1848. From a stereoview by MA Kleckner

Miners Going to Work. Panther Creek Valley, Pa.

Visitors to the region included writers and those whose wealth and position gave them the resources to travel. They visited the town of Mauch Chunk, rode the railroad to the mines, and penned accounts which they carried back home. These stories were very descriptive and emphasized the wild scenery that the railroad passed through, as well as the speed of the cars.

Rather than saddle itself with operation of the passenger service, the company contracted the operation to private individuals, who operated the "Pleasure Carriages," as they came to be known. The first private operator was Joseph Lippincott of Mauch Chunk.

The company originally took as its compensation one half of gross receipts and set the fare at fifty cents for strangers and twenty-five cents for "Mauch Chunkers." Of course, traveling on company business earned one a free ride. The company soon changed the requirement, taking half of net receipts, since only $202.53 was made as profit during the 1828 season. By May of 1829 the fare for strangers was increased to seventy-five cents, and for twenty five cents on each "succeeding trip on the same visit." [289]

As the LC&N Company expanded the mining and shipment of coal, passenger traffic began to interfere with coal shipments. Passenger service was temporarily discontinued in January 1838. The railroad remained free from the passenger coaches until sometime late in 1843 when Alexander McLean, a Summit Hill mine contractor and tavern operator, began a short lived passenger service on the railroad. This was not continued during the 1844 season. [290]

It wasn't until the completion of the return or Back Track, in 1846, that the LC&N restored passenger and tourist traffic on the Summit Hill and Mauch Chunk gravity railroad.

Surprisingly, in May of 1848, while expansion of the railroad and mining into the Panther Creek Valley was in its early stages, the LC&N soon permitted passengers to descend into the valley. A newspaper ad posted by the proprietor of the passenger cars advertised that he was running a service from Mauch Chunk twice a day and that by this arrangement strangers and others have an opportunity of visiting the great Summit Mines of the Lehigh Co . . . also if they desire it, visit the Panther Creek improvements returning to the Summit in time for dinner.[291]

By this time, the first return backtrack into the valley had been completed, and the term "switchback" was soon coined. The first newspaper article discovered that uses the term was the May 29, 1851 edition of the *Carbon County Gazette.*

The Excursion on the Back track & around the "switch backs" in Panther Creek Valley, is truly a delightful one.[292]

The author of the article used the opportunity to comment on the miners housing:

No one can avoid noticing the vast superiority of the miners' dwellings recently erected, not only at the Summit but in all the little villages in the vicinity, over those used in the early days of mining. The new dwellings are neat and commodious; whereas the old ones, not only in the Summit but in Carbondale and other mining villages which we have visited, are hardly fit for human habitations.[293]

Miners Posing in Panther Valley. From the brochure "Souvenir of Mauch Chunk Famous Switchback and Panther Creek Valley," published for John C. Tosh, Mauch Chunk, Pa. Price 25 cents. Circa 1910. John Tosh was the proprietor of a well-known clothing store in Mauch Chunk.

Panther Valley miners pose in front of Tunnel No. 8 sometime in the 1860s. The mine and colliery would eventually become an LC&N showplace. From a stereoview by photographer Joseph Brown.

In 1852 one traveler described the trip into the valley:

> As the cars pass down this valley in the mountains, they are detached at various points, and pass under the coal breakers-grim, dusty, monsters. . . the coal is emptied into the coal breaker, which by means of rollers, crushes it in pieces, and after going through a number of screens, which separated it from dust, and sort it into the various sizes, it passes through several troughs, along which men and boys are seated, busily selecting the slate, as the coal is discharged into the cars beneath.[294]

The Panther Valley and its transportation network posed conspicuous dangers to the miners and laborers, but were even more hazardous to the tourists, who were unfamiliar with the works and with precautions necessary to prevent injuries. It should not be surprising that accidents, some of them fatal, would occur to valley tourists.

On Saturday last several strangers made a pleasure trip over the Switch Back Railroad, and coming up Plane No. 1, on the safety car, one of the party a gentleman residing near Philadelphia stood up and carelessly leaned against a coal car in front, and on reaching the top of the plane the coal car ran on and the safety car stopped which caused him to fall out and badly break his leg below the knee. He was taken to Harris' Hotel where he immediately received medical attendance. He will probably remain laid up for some weeks.[295]

Mauch Chunk and Summit Hill
RAIL-ROAD.
CHANGE OF TIME! ON AND AF- ter Wednesday, June 1, 1859. the trains will run as follows:

Leave foot of Mount Pisgah at 8 A. M. and 3. P. M.
Leave Summit Hill at 11 A. M. and 5½ P. M.

On arriving at the Summit, morning and afternoon, trips will be made around the Switch-Back, for the accommodation of Passengers.

STEWART M. LINE, Conductor.
Mauch Chunk, June 9, 1859.

From the *Mauch Chunk Gazette*
2 Jun 1859, DML

115

A loaded coal car waits at the bottom of Panther Creek Plane No. 2. The Panther Valley inclined planes hoisted both loaded coal cars as well as passenger cars, presenting dangerous conditions to tourists. The culm banks visible at the top left are probably the spoil banks from Slope No. 2. From a stereoview by MA Kleckner.

To be accommodative at times the LC&N even allowed touring of the mines:

On reaching Breaker No. 6, Mr. Douglas, who accompanied the party, kindly tendered all who desired, an opportunity to enter the Mine, which was gladly accepted, this being the least wet or disagreeable of any in the region. A truck and Mule was at once procured, and our party, in Company with Messrs. Murphy, Sisty and Bertsch, and "Bob," the driver, at once proceeded in, five hundred and some feet, till we came to a very interesting settlement. Here they have a powerful steam Engine, hundreds of feet below ground, and everything remarkably dry and comfortable to those engaged there. They even have the interior around the Engine whitewashed.

116

We next passed through No. 6 Breaker. Several of our party saw the operations for the first time, and seemed very much interested. Our next stopping place was the New Breaker, No. 9, just completed, with all the latest improvements. It was used for the first time this week.[296]

A trip around the Summit Hill and Mauch Chunk gravity railroad, including descent into the Panther Creek valley, took on average less than 4 hours. Although early trips allowed examination of the No. 6 colliery, soon the Coaldale No. 8 colliery became the preferred colliery for tourists.

As one writer noted:

In the valley of Panther Creek, beyond Summit Village, we pause for fifteen minutes to take a peep into the cavernous entrance to Coal Dale Mine, No. 8, a dark, damp, dangerous-looking hole in the side of the hill, from which come ominous gleams of light and a heavy stream of air which chills us to our bones.[297]

The LC&N rarely operated the passenger cars, instead leased or contracted out that privilege. Fisher Hazard (1829 – 1888) son of LC&N co-founder Erskine Hazard operated the "Pleasure Carriages" on the Switchback from 1860 to 1863, paying an annual fee of $750 for the privilege. Hazard also operated the Company's wire rope factory in Mauch Chunk. Panther Valley No. 9 Mine Museum

The decade of the 1860s saw many strikes and worker "turnouts" in the Panther Valley region. In addition, planned work suspensions, today known as layoffs, occurred when the LC&N along with other coal companies attempted to raise the price of coal by reducing the supply. When this occurred, passenger trains into the valley stopped running, while the original gravity railroad continued to bring passengers into Summit Hill.[298]

On one occasion in 1862, when tourists were not permitted to descend into the Panther Creek Valley, the proprietor protested to the LC&N managers.

"A letter from the Chief Clerk states that 'Fisher Hazard claims a reduction of the amount charged him under the lease to run passenger cars on the Summit Rail Road, for 1862, in view of his being deprived of the use of one third of the distance viz the Panther Creek rail road for four months.' In consideration of which it was, OMR, that he be allowed a deduction of ninety dollars." [299]

On one occasion, in 1869, a tourist reported

"The miners suspended operations on the 8th of May last, and have not yet resumed, so that the town swarms with crowds of men and boys for whose idle hands the Devil, as is his wont, finds plenty of work." [300]

In the early 1870s the cost of riding the famed Mauch Chunk gravity railroad to Summit Hill and back was 75 cents, with an additional 50 cents tacked on to make the trip into the Panther Valley.[301]

The summer season of 1872 very heavy coal traffic over the original gravity railroads, and the LC&N saw the need to terminate most passenger traffic into the valley

Many supposed that this was sharp practice on the part of the officers of the road, and naturally felt indignant. The cause for the taking off of passenger trains over this part of the route is this: The Lehigh Coal and Navigation Company use the same track for the shipping of coal from their numerous breakers. The trains during the day are numerous, and as no schedule time can be made for running them, there was great danger of passenger and coal trains colliding. *As no accident has yet happened to any passenger on this road*, the officers, with their usual precaution, deemed it best to stop passenger trains at Summit Hill, charging tourists 75 cts. instead of $1.25 for the round trip. We think the public will gain instead of losing by this change; the ride through the Panther Creek Valley has no attractions save the mines and coal breakers, whereas by remaining at Summit Hill half an hour or more all this can be seen, besides viewing the wonderful burning mine, the place where Philip Ginter first discovered coal, and numerous other attractions.[302] (Author's Emphasis)

In December of 1872 the last coal train rolled down the Summit Hill and Mauch Chunk gravity railroad to the coal schutes on the Lehigh River. That marked the end of the Switchback as a coal hauler. It also marked the end of the Panther Valley Switchback as a tourist attraction. However, tourists would continue to flock to Mauch Chunk and Summit Hill and ride the original gravity railroad well into the 20th century.

Panther Valley Tunnel No. 8 and Coal Breaker. From Lippincott's Magazine of *Popular Literature and Science*, August 1872. "A Switchback Excursion."

Appendix B
Pennsylvania's Panther Creek Valley and
The origin of the Railroad term "Switch-Back"

This author has researched and written about the Summit Hill and Mauch Chunk gravity railroad since 1970. So it was recently a great surprise to learn that, in all likelihood, the famous Summit Hill and Mauch Chunk Switchback Railroad led to the ubiquitous use of the railroad term "Switch-Back."

This author cannot take credit for this discovery. That distinction goes to Christopher Northington, who spends his time at the Genealogy Desk at the Dimmick Memorial Library. Besides writing and genealogy, Chris is also interested in etymology, and was curious enough about the term "switch-back" to discover that it originated from our area's famous railroad.

After learning of Chris' discovery, I went back into my own research and learned that the term did not show up in LC&N records until 1854, when the LC&N Board of Managers authorized construction of a "switch-back" to connect the Hacklebernie Tunnel with the Summit Hill and Mauch Chunk gravity railroad.

Through on-line research Chris discovered that the first time the term appeared in national newspapers was in the August 5, 1852 issue of the *Philadelphia Public Ledger,* in a letter to the editor from a correspondent who had braved a trip down the soon-to-be famous railroad:

> The cars are then driven by gravity for three fourths of a mile, to "Summit Hill," a collection of mining villages, numbering about 1200 inhabitants. They then thunder down a zig zag road four and a half miles in length, called from its peculiar arrangement, the "Switch-Back," varying in its grades from two hundred and thirty four to fifty feet, in the mile.

This author's research turned up the fact that on May 29, 1851, three years after the construction of the first set of switches, the term had first appeared locally in the *Carbon County Gazette*, a Mauch Chunk newspaper:

> Those who have never done so, should improve the present opportunity to visit the "old mines." The Excursion on the Back track & around the "switch backs" in Panther Creek Valley, is truly a delightful one.

Taking his research even deeper, Chris discovered that the Oxford English Dictionary had identified the Panther Creek Switch-Back as the origin of the word, citiing an article in the September 1863 issue of *Harper's Magazine* entitled "The Pennsylvania Coal Region" describing a visit to the Panther Creek Valley.

> We descend from our high elevation by gravity, changing our direction at various points by means of what is called a Switch-back.

By 1890 the term was in use figuratively in American English.

Appendix C
Operation of the "Switch-Back" Switches

No information has as yet been uncovered in LC&N records concerning the design and operation of the famous Switchback Railroad switches, however, from various descriptions penned by travelers on the railroad, we can deduce some facts concerning their operation. (Refer to the following diagram and the diagram on the facing page).

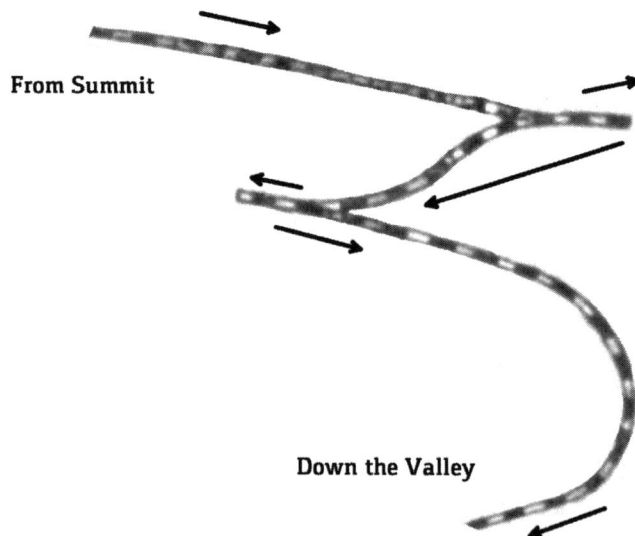

From Summit

Down the Valley

Adapted from Springvale section of 1854 Philip Nunan Map

The early design of the Panther Valley switchback had two backtracks into the valley for empty cars. Each backtrack had a set of 2 switches, forming a switch-back.

A descending car entered the first of the switches, its momentum along with the car wheels and rigid axles forcing open switch points, allowing the car to pass through. Once through the switch the car moved along an ascending grade on the "tail" track, the length and elevation of which was designed to remove some, if not all of the momentum of the car. When the momentum was exhausted, either before or at the bumper, the car reversed direction and descended through the the open points of the first switch, to the next switch, where the action repeated. After passing through both switches of a "switch-back" the car headed lower into the valley.

The movable rails containing the switch points were attached to a "throw" bar that was only attached to a "spring device" which we must assume was similar to a leaf spring. The spring was itself attached to an immovable support, proababy a wooden tie attached to the non-movable rails.

The following are notable facts:
- The switch "tail" was as long as possible to increase friction of tracks.
- Cars entering the "tail" moved uphill, cars leaving the "tail" moved downhill.
- The switch points were long enough so that trains of several cars could pass through the switch.
- Once the last car had passed through the points and was located in the tail, the switch points reclosed, allowing the cars to coast back through the switch which was now open in the downhill direction toward the next switch or the valley floor.

From Summit or previous switch

To next switch or lower in the valley

The switch is shown in the "normal" position. Descending cars with significant momentum, reposition the moveable rails, i.e. "points" against spring pressure, allowing the cars to pass through the switch, toward the bumper on the "tail" track.

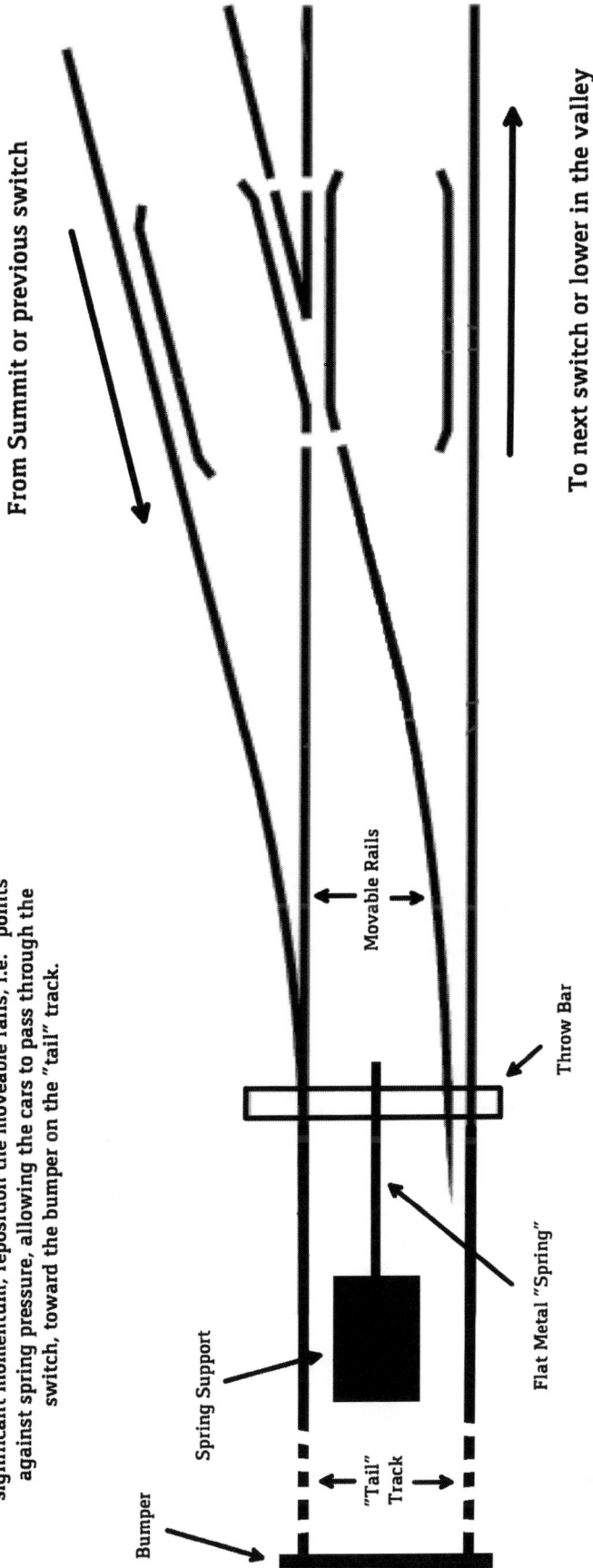

After the cars pass through the switch along the "tail" toward the bumper, the spring repositions the moveable rails, i.e. the "points" to allow the cars, with significantly lower momentum, to pass through to the next switch or down into the valley.

Movable Rails

Throw Bar

Flat Metal "Spring"

Spring Support

Bumper

"Tail" Track

Appendix D
Panther Valley Coal Production (includes Summit Hill Mines)
From LC&N Annual Report 4 May 1869, Table of Coal Production

Year	Tonnage
1847	201,951
1848	214,839
1849	276,501
1850	330,447
1851	393,353
1852	429,786
1853	393,255
1854	413,049
1855	312,354
1856	284,711
1857	316,411
1858	284,704
1859	402,030
1860	386,452
1861	322,917
1862	185,061
1863	380,302
1864	347,982
1865	400,460
1866	408,243
1867	370,204
1868	387,220
1869	412,609
1870	261,187
1871	462,128
1872	498,866
1873	451,549
1874	572,617
1875	397,338

Endnotes

The following conventions are used in these notes:
CHTP: Canal History and Technology Press and its predecessor, Center for Canal History and Technology (the publishing department of the National Canal Museum).
DML: Dimmick Memorial Library, Jim Thorpe, PA.
LC&N: Lehigh Coal and Navigation Company

1 Alfred Mathews and Austin Hungerford, *History of the Counties of Lehigh and Carbon in the Commonwealth of Pennsylvania* (Philadelphia: Everts and Richards, 1884), 573.

2 H. Benjamin Powell, *Philadelphia's First Fuel Crisis: Jacob Cist and the Developing Market for Pennsylvania Anthracite* (University Park: The Pennsylvania State University Press, 1978), 12.

3 Philip Ginder Land Warrant, Pennsylvania Historical and Museum Commission State Archives, Record Group RG-17.

4 George Korson, *Black Rock: Mining Folklore of the Pennsylvania Dutch* (Baltimore: The Johns Hopkins Press, 1960), 9.

5 Christopher Baer, "White and Hazard and the Lehigh Coal and Navigation Company, 1804-1840." Unpublished Manuscript, 1983, in National Canal Museum Library and Archives, Easton, PA.

6 Joseph Mortimer Levering, *A History of Bethlehem, Pennsylvania 1741-1892* (Bethlehem: Times Publishing Company, 1903), 541.

7 Lehigh Coal Mine Company Meeting Minutes (LCMC), Pennsylvania Historical and Museum Commission, MG-311, Microfilm Roll 11, 28 Feb 1803.

8 Levering, *History of Bethlehem, Pennsylvania,* 546.

9 Powell, *Philadelphia's First Fuel Crisis,* 10.

10 *Mauch Chunk Democrat,* 6 Feb 1875, DML.

11 LC&N Annual Report, 4 May 1869.

12 *Lehigh Pioneer and Mauch Chunk Courier,* 16 Jan 1841, DML.

13 LC&N Annual Report, 9 Jan 1843, 5-6.

14 *Mauch Chunk Coal Gazette,* 12 Jul 1841, DML.

15 Samuel Harries Daddow and Benjamin Banaan, *Coal, Iron, and Oil; or, the Practical American Miner* (Pottsville, 1866), 871.

16 LC&N Annual Report, 9 Jan 1843, 7.

17 Jacob Cist Collection, Luzerne County Historical Society, Wilkes-Barre, Pa.

18 LC&N Annual Report, 11 Jan 1830, 13.

19 *Mauch Chunk Democrat,* 30 Dec 30, 1899, DML.

20 Samuel T. Wiley, *Biographical and Portrait Cyclopedia of Schuylkill County, Pennsylvania* (Philadelphia, Rush, West and Company, 1893) 27, 168.

21 LC&N Annual Report, 13 Jan 1840, 24.

22 LC&N Executive Committee Minutes, 21 Oct 1840.

23 *Carbon County Gazette,* 7 Aug 1844, DML.

24 Mathews and Hungerford, *History,* 790; Richard J. Hoben, *Lansford the First One Hundred Years* (Lansford, PA, 1976), 7-9.

25 Horace E. Hayden and Alfred Hand, *Genealogical and Family History of Wyoming and Lackawanna Valleys,* Vol I. (Pennsylvania, 1906), 178-179.

26 Ibid.

27 LC&N Managers Minutes, 23 Mar 1842.

28 *Mauch Chunk Courier,* 3 Apr 1841; LC&N Managers Minutes, 9 May 1834.

29 *Mauch Chunk Democrat,* 3 May 1879, DML.

30 Muriel Sibell Wolle, *Montana Pay Dirt: A Guide to the Mining Camps of the Treasure State* (Denver: Sage Books 1963), 61.

31 Hayden and Hand, *Wyoming and Lackawanna History,* 179.

32 LC&N Managers Minutes, 17 Aug 1843.

33 LC&N Executive Committee Minutes, 22 Sep 1843.

34 LC&N Executive Committee Minutes, 14 Dec 1843.

35 *Carbon County Gazette,* 26 Jun 1844; 14 Aug 1844, DML; LC&N Managers Minutes, 16 \Aug 1844.

36   LC&N Managers Minutes, 31 Jan 31 1844.

37   Robert Heysham Sayre, Personal Diary, 16 Apr 1851, National Cana Museum Library and Archives, Easton, Pa.

38   LC&N Annual Report, 13 Jan 1845, 8.

39   LC&N Managers Minutes, 31 Dec, 1844.

40   LC&N Managers Minutes, 14 Dec 1843.

41   LC&N Managers Minutes 9, Jan 1844.

42   LC&N Annual Report, 13 Jan 1845, 8.

43   LC&N Annual Report 5 May 1846, 8.

44   *Mauch Chunk Coal Gazette* 15 Jul 1892, DML.

45   LC&N Executive Committee Minutes, 5 Aug 1844.

46   Katharine Foster Thompson, *Chapter and Verse: The Annotated Diaries of Asa Lansford Foster (1798-1868)* (Wilmington, DE, 1992), 339; *Carbon County Gazette*, 15 May 1844, DML.

47   Fred Brenckman, *History of Carbon County* (Harrisburg: James J. Nungesser, 1913), 282.

48   Thompson, *Chapter and Verse*, 271-272; *Mauch Chunk Gazette*, 8 Dec 1853, DML.

49   LC&N Executive Committee Minutes 9 Jan 1844, 5 Aug 1844, 11 Dec 1844; *Carbon County Gazette* 9 Jan 1845, DML.

50   Letter from Moncure Robinson to LC&N Board of Managers, LC&N Managers Minutes, 21 Dec 1829.

51   *Carbon County Gazette,* 14 Aug 1845, DML.

52   LC&N Managers Minutes, 24 Sep 1845.

53   LC&N Executive Committee Minutes, 22 Oct 1845.

54   LC&N Managers Minutes, 12 Nov 1845; *Carbon County Gazette* 20 Nov 1845; 30 Oct 1845., DML.

55   LC&N Managers Minutes, 12 Nov 1845.

56   Thompson, *Chapter and Verse*, 4-5.

57   Mathews and Hungerford, *History*, 672, 700.

58   Thompson, *Chapter and Verse*, 4-5, 272.

59   *Carbon County Gazette*, 30, Sept 1852, 21 Oct 1852., DML.

60   Hoben, *Lansford's First One Hundred Years*, 11.

61   LC&N Managers Minutes, 12 Nov 1845; Mathews and Hungerford, *History*, 703, 741.

62   *Carbon Democrat*, 14 May 1864; LC&N Annual Report 1 May 1866, 36.

63   *Carbon Democrat*, 20 Jul 1889, DML.

64   *Mauch Chunk Courier*, 11 Jun 1838; LC&N Managers Minutes, 12 Nov 1845; 22 Dec 1847; 2 Jan 1850; *Carbon Democrat*. 24 Nov 1849, DML.

65   LC&N Managers Minutes, 5 Aug 1844; *Carbon County Gazette*, 12 Dec 1844; Thompson, *Chapter and Verse*, 395.

66   Thompson, *Chapter and Verse*, 395.

67   Mathews and Hungerford, *History*, 672; *Carbon Democrat*, 20 Feb 20 1873; LC&N Executive Committee Minutes, 1 Feb 1832.

68   *County Atlas of Carbon Pennsylvania* From actual Surveys by and Under the Direction of F. W. Beers (New York, Charles Hart, 1875), 49.

69   Mathews and Hungerford, *History*, 674.

70   LC&N Executive Committee Minutes, 29 Nov 1836.

71   *Mauch Chunk Democrat*, 6 Feb 1875; *Mauch Chunk Courier*, 17 Apr 1837, DML.

72   *Mauch Chunk Democrat*, 6 Feb 1875, DML.

73   *Wilkes-Barre Telephone*, 13 Feb 1886; *Carbon Democrat*, 14 Jul 1849, 20 Jul 1850, DML.

74   *Mauch Chunk Courier*, 18 Oct 1841; Thompson, *Chapter and Verse*, 288; LC&N Executive Committee Minutes, 1 Feb 1832.

75   John N. Hoffman, *Anthracite in the Lehigh Valley of Pennsylvania 1820-45* (Washington, D.C.: Smithsonian Institution Press, 1968, 108-109, "Map of the Mount Pisgah Backtrack and Summit Rail Road, Line of the Proposed Panther Creek Railroad, January 1845."

76   "Draft of 11,000 Acres of Iron and Coal Land in the Hazelton and Beaver Meadow or Second Anthracite Coal Field in Schuylkill and Luzerne Counties Pennsylvania." The Estate of John Hare Powel, Esq. Surveyed 1845 by W. F. Roberts, Engineer of Mines and Colliery Viewer, RG-17, Pennsylvania Canal Maps, Map Book #1, Pennsylvania State Archives, Harrisburg.

77   Jay Frantz, "Tracking down details of the Number 4 Plane" Lansford *Valley Gazette*, Jan 1976, 5-7.

78   LC&N Annual Report, 21 Apr 1848, 24.

79   LC&N Managers Minutes, 4 No, 1846.

80   LC&N Executive Committee Minutes, 5 Jul 1848.

81   LC&N Annual Report, 4 May 1847, 9.

82   LC&N Annual Report 4 May 1847, 6.

83   Mathews and Hungerford, *History*, 673.

84   Gerald Bastoni, "Episodes from the Life of Canvass White Pioneer American Civil Engineer," Canal History and Technology Proceedings, Vol. I, 1982, 58.

85   As found on headstone for Charles Loomis White in Upper Mauch Chunk Cemetery, Jim Thorpe, PA; https://www.findagrave.com/memorial/67003399/charles-loomis-white, accessed 10 Jun 2021.

86   *Carbon County Gazette*, 26 Aug 1852, DML.

87   Vincent Hydro, Jr., "Mauch Chunk as an Anthracite Coal Mining Town," Canal History and Technology Proceedings, Vol. XI, 1992, 85.

88   Thompson, *Chapter and Verse*, 229-230; *Carbon Democrat*, 17 Jun 1854, DML.

89   *Carbon County Gazette & Mauch Chunk Courier*, 15 Feb 1849, DML.

90   LC&N Managers Minutes, 7 Jun 1843, 5 Oct 1843, 19 Nov 1845, 7 Sep 1849, 21 Jan 1852, 22 Dec 1852, 21 Jun 1854, 24 Jan 1855.

91   LC&N Executive Committee Minutes at Mauch Chunk, 1 Jul 1841.

92   *Carbon Democrat*, 7 May 1853, DML.

93   LC&N Managers Minutes, 29 Aug 1860.

94   Robert H. Sayre, Diary Entry, 31 Dec 1851.

95   LC&N Annual Report, 2 May 1848, 20-21.

96   Vince Hydro, *History of the Lehigh Coal and Navigation Company Series: The Room Run Gravity Railroad, with an Early History of Nesquehoning* (Jim Thorpe: Vince Hydro Publications, 2019), 39.

97   Ibid.

98   LC&N Annual Report, 2 May 1848, 21-22.

99   *Carbon County Gazette and Mauch Chunk Courier*, 20 Mar 1851.

100   LC&N Managers Minutes, 22 Dec 22 1847; *Carbon County Gazette*, 2 Sep 1847, DML.

101   Robert H. Sayre, Diary Entry, 5-6 May 1852.

102   *Carbon County Gazette*, 4 Mar 1847, DML.

103   LC&N Managers Minutes, 18 Nov 1846.

104   M.S. Henry, *History of the Lehigh Valley* (Easton: Bixler and Corwin, 1860), 354.

105   LC&N Managers Minutes, 22 Dec 1847; *Carbon County Gazette*, 2 Sep 1847, DML.

106   Ibid.

107   *Carbon County Gazette*, 25 May 1848, DML.

108   LC&N Annual Report, 2 May 1848; 1 May 1849.

109   As noted by Walt Niehoff in an email to the author dated 1 Apr 2000.

110   *Mauch Chunk Gazette,* 28 Oct 1858, DML.

111   LC&N Annual Report, 7 May 1850, 19.

112   LC&N Managers Minutes, 13 Oct 1847.

113   Donald Sayenga, "The Early Years of America's Wire Rope Industry 1818-1848," Canal History and Technology Proceedings, Vol. X., 1991, 135.

114   *Carbon County Gazette,* 13 Jul 1848, DML.

115   LC&N Annual Report, 1 May 1849, 20.

116   Henry Darwin Rogers, *The Geology of Pennsylvania* (Philadelphia, J.B. Lippincott, 1858), 72-73.

117   Robert H. Sayre, Diary Entry, 31 Dec 1851.

118   LC&N Annual Report, 1 May 1849, 20-21.

119   *Carbon Democrat*, 4 Apr 1863, DML.

120   *Mauch Chunk Gazette*, 1 Apr 1858, DML.

121   LC&N Annual Report, 1 May 1849, 22.

122   LC&N Annual Report 1 May 1849, 8.

123   LC&N Annual Report 1 May 1849, 21.

124   Ibid.

125   LC&N Annual Report, 2 May1848, 23.

126   LC&N Annual Report, 1 May 1849, 21.

127   LC&N Annual Report, 2 May 1848, 23.

128   LC&N Managers Minutes 22 Dec 1847.

129   LC&N Managers Minutes, 2 Jan 1850.

130   LC&N Managers Minutes, 6 Dec 1855.

131   LC&N Annual Report, 5 May 1863, 59.

132   *Mauch Chunk Gazette*, 5 Nov 1863, DML.

133   *Mauch Chunk Gazette*, 4 Feb 1864., DML.

134   LC&N Annual Report, 1 May 1849, 22.

135   LC&N Annual Report, 7 May 1850, 19.

136   Henry Darwin Rogers, *Geology*, 71-73.

137   LC&N Annual Report, 7 May 1850, 19.

138   LC&N Annual Report, 7 May 1850, 8.

139   LC&N Managers Minutes, 2 Jan 1850; 7 Sep 1849; 24 Oct 1849.

140   LC&N Managers Minutes, 7 Sep 1849.

141   *Carbon County Gazette and Mauch Chunk Courier*, 15 Jul 1847, DML.

142   LC&N Managers Minutes, 3 July 1849.

143   Ibid.

144   Robert H. Sayre, personal diaries, various entries.

145   *Mauch Chunk Gazette*, 24 May 1860, DML.

146   M.S. Henry, *History*, 354.

147   Map of the Counties of Monroe and Carbon Pennsylvania. From surveys under the direction of H.F. Walling. Published by Loomis Way & Palmer, 1860; *Evening Telegraph*, 25 Jun 1869.

148   Walter Niehoff, II. Personal email to the author on 1 Apr 2000.

149   LC&N Managers Minutes, 28 August 1850.

150   LC&N Annual Report, 6 May 1851, 21.

151   LC&N Annual Report, 6 May 1851, 22-23.

152   *Mauch Chunk Coal Gazette*, 26 Apr 1895; Thompson, *Chapter and Verse*, 376-377.

153   *Carbon Democrat*, 7 Sep 1850, DML.

154   Findagrave.com lists Lucy Waller Abbott as the first burial in Mauch Chunk Cemetery. Cemetery records list date of her death as 1819 but other sources give date as 22 May 1822.

155   LC&N Managers Minutes, 10 Jan 1837; *Philadelphia Inquirer,* 31 Jan 1874.

156   Mathews and Hungerford, *History*, 790.

157   Lansford *Valley Gazette*, Aug 1977, 5.

158   LC&N Managers Minutes, 8 Jun 1859.

159   *Philadelphia Inquirer*, 7 Jan 1874.

160   *Carbon Democrat*, 3 Jun 1865; 17 Jun 1865, DML.

161   *Mauch Chunk Democrat*, 31 Jan 1874, DML.

162   *Carbon County Gazette*, 1 Jul 1847, DML.

163   *Carbon Democrat*, 4 Jan 1851, DML.

164   *Carbon County Gazette*, 4 Sep 1851; 13 May 1858, DML.

165   LC&N Managers Minutes, 26 Dec 1860.

166   LC&N Annual Report, 5 May 1863, 59-60.

167   *Mauch Chunk Gazette*, 4 Sep 1862; *Carbon Democrat*, 17 Jan 1863, DML.

168   *Carbon County Gazette*, 4 Sep 1851, DML.

169   LC&N Managers Minutes, 23 Mar 1859.

170   Thompson, *Chapter and Verse*, 265; *Mauch Chunk Gazette*, 25 Sep 1862, DML.

171   *Hazleton Plain Speaker*, 14 Feb 1902.

172   *Lehigh Pioneer and Mauch Chunk Courier*, 18 Oct 1834; LC&N Exec Committee Minutes 29 Nov 1836.

173   *Mauch Chunk Courier*, 5 Jun 1837, DML.

174   *Mauch Chunk Courier*, 1 Jun 1839; LC&N Managers Minutes 21 Jan 1846; *Carbon Democrat* 30 Nov 1850, DML.

175   Robert F. Archer, *A History of the Lehigh Valley Railroad* (Berkeley: Howell-North Books, 1977), 29.

176   Mathews and Hungerford, *History,* 673.

177   *Mauch Chunk Democrat*, 25 Nov 1876; LCN Exec Committee Minutes, 20 Dec 1843; *Allentown Leader*, 27 Jan 1896.

178   Robert H. Sayre, personal diaries, various entries.

179   Ibid, entry for 6 Aug 1851.

180   Frank Whelan and Lance Metz, *The Diaries of Robert Heysham Sayre* (Lehigh University 1990), 7.

181   *Lehigh Pioneer and Mauch Chunk Courier*, 30 Apr 1832, DML.

182   *Mauch Chunk Gazette*, 5 Aug 1858, DML.

183   Mathews and Hungerford, *History*, 671; *Carbon Democrat*, 22 Apr 1848, DML.

184   *Carbon County Gazette*, 10 Jul 1851; Mathews and Hungerford, *History*, 671.

185   Robert H. Sayre, Diary, 22 Oct 1851.

186   Henry Darwin Rogers, *Geology*, 74-75.

187   Ibid.

188   Ibid.

189   Ibid.

190   LC&N Annual Report, 4 May 1852, 8; 3 May 1853, 11.

191   Anthony Brzyski, "The Lehigh Canal and its Effect on the Economic Development of the Region Through Which it Passed" 1818-1873, (unpublished Ph.D. dissertation, NY University, 1957), 640.

192   LC&N Managers Minutes, 1 Jan 14, 1852; 1 Jan 21, 1852; 26 Mar 1852.

193   LC&N Annual Report, 2 May 1854, 18.

194   LC&N Annual Report, 4 May 1858, 19; *Mauch Chunk Gazette*, 29 Apr 1858, DML.

195   https://no9minemuseum.wixsite.com/museum/about-us

196   LC&N Managers Minutes 13 Oct 1847; LC&N Annual Report, 2 May 1854, 18.

197   LC&N Annual Report, 1 May 1855, 22.

198   LC&N Annual Report, 6 May 1856, 20; 4 May 1869, Table of Coal Production.

199   LC&N Managers Minutes, 12 Dec 22, 1847.

200   Thompson, *Chapter and Verse*, 5.

201   Ibid; *Mauch Chunk Coal Gazette*, 26 Apr 1895, *Mauch Chunk Democrat*, 20 Aug 1870.

202   LC&N Managers Minutes, 10 Jan 1855.

203   LC&N Managers Minutes, 16 May 1855.

204   LC&N Managers Minutes, 17 Jan 1856.

205   LC&N Annual Report, 1 May 1855, 22.

206   Ibid.

207   LC&N Annual Report, 6 May 1856, 20; 5 May 1857, 19.

208   LC&N Annual Reports for years 1854 through 1858.

209   *Mauch Chunk Gazette*, 9 Jul 1857; 6 Aug 1857, DML.

210   *Mauch Chunk Gazette*, 1 Oct 1857, DML.

211   *Carbon Democrat*, 6 Feb 1858, DML.

212   LC&N Annual Report, 3 May 1859, 8-9.

213   Ibid, 8-11.

214   *Carbon Democrat*, 10 Apr 1858, DML.

215   *Mauch Chunk Gazette*, 22 Apr 1858; *Carbon Democrat*, 24 Apr 1858, DML.

216   LC&N Managers Minutes, 28 Apr 1858.

217   *Mauch Chunk Gazette*, 22 Apr 1858, DML

218   Ibid, 13 May 1858, DML.

219   *Carbon County Gazette*, 4 Sep 1851, DML.

220   LC&N Managers Minutes, 15 Sep 1858.

221   LC&N Annual Report, 3 May 1859, 19.

222   LC&N Managers Minutes, 23 Mar 1859.

223   LC&N Annual Report, 1 May 1860, 20; 3 May 1861, 20.

224   LC&N Annual Report, 1 May 1860, 21.

225   LC&N Managers Minutes, 6 Jul 1859; 20 Jul 1859; 2 Nov 1859.

226   LC&N Annual Report, 1 May 1860, 21.

227   LC&N Managers Minutes, 28 Dec 1859.

228   *Mauch Chunk Coal Gazette*, 2 Feb 1860, DML.

229   LC&N Managers Minutes, 8 Feb 1860.

230   John Leisenring, letter to LC&N Board of Managers, LC&N Managers Minutes, 14 Mar 1860.

231   LC&N Manages Minutes, 14 Mar 1860.

232   LC&N Managers Minutes, 26 Sep 1860.

233   LC&N Managers Minutes, 26 Aug 1857, 31 Mar 1858.

234   LC&N Managers Minutes, 2 Feb 1859.

235   LC&N Annual Report, 5 May 1862, 29.

236   LC&N Managers Minutes, 21 Aug 1861.

237   J.D. Laciar, *Patriotism of Carbon County* (Mauch Chunk, 1867), 60-61, *Carbon County Gazette*, 4 Sep 1851.

238   Thompson, *Chapter and Verse,* 286-287. J.D. Laciar, *Patriotism,* 60-61.

239   LC&N Annual Report, 6 May 1862, 14.

240   *Mauch Chunk Gazette*, 26 Sep 1861, DML.

241   LC&N Annual Report, 5 May 1863, 56-57.

242   LC&N Managers Minutes, 17 Dec 1862.

243   LC&N Managers Minutes, 7 Jan 1863.

244   LC&N Managers Minutes, 7 Jan 1863.

245   LC&N Managers Minutes, 21 Jan 1863.

246   LC&N Annual Report, 3 May 1864, 28.

247   LC&N Managers Minutes, 29 Apr 1863; 15 Jul 1863; 16 Sep 1863; 14 Oct 1863.

248   *Carbon Democrat*, 12 Sep 1863, DML.

249   LC&N Managers Minutes, 18 Nov 1863.

250   Ibid.

251   Ibid.

252   Letter from, John Leisenring to Richard Richardson, Norris Hansell, *Josiah White Quaker Entrepreneur* (Easton, PA: CHTP, 1992), 105.

253   LC&N Annual Report 1 May 1866, 8-9.

254   LC&N Managers Minutes, 27 Dec 1865.

255   LC&N Annual Report, 1 May 1866, 19.

256   LC&N Annual Report, 5 May 1868, 46.

257   LC&N Annual Report, 1 May 1866, 31-32.

258   "The Story of St. Mary's, Coaldale, Pa. Souvenir Record, $7,500 Parish Campaign, 1918." https://www.coaldale-alumni.com/StoryofStMarys1918.pdf)

259   Vince Hydro, *Room Run History*, 65-66

260   *Carbon Democrat*, 16 May 1868, DML.

261   *Carbon Democrat,* 13 June 1868, DML.

262   *Carbon Democrat*, 8 Aug 1868, DML.

263   LC&N Annual Report, 4 May 1869, 26.

264   *Carbon Democrat*, 29 Feb 1872, DML.

265   *Mauch Chunk Democrat*, 14 Oct 1876, DML.

266   LC&N Managers Minutes, 27 Dec 1865, LC&N Annual Report, 7 May 1867, 36.

267   LC&N Annual Report, 7 May 1867, 33.

268   *Carbon Democrat*, 7 Apr 1866, DML.

269   *Carbon Democrat*, 26 May 1866; LC&N Managers Minutes 30 May 1866.

270   LC&N Managers Minutes 5 Jul 1866.

271   *Carbon Democrat*, 18 Aug 1866, DML.

272   LC&N Managers Minutes, 25 Mar 1868; 8 Apr 1868; 6 May 1868.

273   LC&N Annual Report, 4 May 1869, 4.

274   LC&N Annual Report 4 May 1869, 16 Jan 1869.

275   LC&N Annual Report 4 May 1869.

276   *Carbon Democrat*, 19 Mar 1870, DML.

277   LC&N Annual Report, 2 May 1871, 7; LC&N Annual Report, 3 May 1870, 15.

278   *Mauch Chunk Coal Gazette*, 9 Feb 1872, DML.

279   *Mauch Chunk Coal Gazette*, 1 Nov 1872, DML.

280   *Mauch Chunk Coal Gazette*; 21 June 1872; Hoben, *Lansford One Hundred Years*, 87, 112.

281   *Mauch Chunk Coal Gazette*, 21 Mar 1873, DML.

282   *Mauch Chunk Coal Gazette*, 16 Oct 1891, DML.

283   *Mauch Chunk Democrat*, May 13, 1876, DML.

284   *Carbon Democrat*, 11 Jun 1870, DML

285   *Mauch Chunk Democrat*, 15 Dec 1877; *Mauch Chunk Coal Gazette*, 4 Jan 1878, DML.

286   LC&N Annual Report, 23 Feb 1875, 5; *Mauch Chunk Democrat*, 4 Jul 1874, DML.

287   LC&N Annual Report, 25 Feb 1872.

288   Pottsville *Miners' Journal*, 2 June 1827.

289   LC&N Managers Minutes, 3 Feb 1829; 22 May 1829; *Lehigh Pioneer and Mauch Chunk Courier*,
       27 Aug 1829.

290   The last ad for passenger service over the railroad was in *Mauch Chunk Courier*, 1 Jan 1838.

291   *Carbon County Gazette*, 25 May 1848, DML.

292   Ibid, 29 May 1851.

293   Ibid.

294   Ibid, 5 Aug 1852.

295   *Mauch Chunk Coal Gazette*, 25 Jun 1857, DML.

296   *Mauch Chunk Gazette*, 29 Apr 1858, DML.

297   *Philadelphia Evening Telegraph*, 25 Jun 1869.

298   *Carbon Democrat*, 13 Apr 1867, DML.

299   LC&N Board of Managers Minutes 21 Jan 1863.

300   *Philadelphia Evening Telegraph*, 25 Jun 1869.

301   *Mauch Chunk Democrat*, 15 Jun 1872, DML.

302   *Mauch Chunk Democrat*, 3 Aug 1872, DML..

In *Summit Hill and Panther Creek Operations & the Switch-Back Railroad* historian and author Vince Hydro relates the history of Lehigh Coal and Navigation Company mining and railroad operations in Summit Hill, Pennsylvania, and the Panther Creek Valley, including the section of the famous Summit Hill and Mauch Chunk Switch-Back gravity railroad. The early use of the ingenious "Switch-Backs" in the valley gave the railroad its famous name and drew countless tourists to the region.

Vince Hydro, a native of Carbon County, Pennsylvania, continues to write extensively on Carbon County history, Mauch Chunk, and the Lehigh Coal and Navigation Company. His acclaimed book: *The Mauch Chunk Switchback: America's Pioneer Railroad*, was published by the Canal History and Technology Press in 2002. In 2019 Hydro published *The History of the Lehigh Coal & Navigation Company's Room Run Railroad*, the LC&N's second gravity railroad.

ISBN 978-1-7923-9553-6

90000>

9 781792 395536